Enhancing the Library System

donated by the

LIBRARY FOUNDATION
OF MARTIN COUNTY

WHERE THE HELL HAVE YOU BEEN?

WHERE THE HELL HAVE YOU BEEN?

TOM CARVER

First published in 2009 by

Short Books
3A Exmouth House
Pine Street
EC1R 0JH

10 9 8 7 6 5 4 3

A CIP catalogue record for this book is available from the British Library.

ISBN 978-1-906021-53-5

Printed in Great Britain by Clays, Suffolk

Photographs on pages 27, 52, 55
courtesy of the Imperial War Museum, London

Cover design: Emily Fox

**To Katty
and the next generation: Felix, Maya, Jude & Poppy
with much love.**

"There is always one moment in childhood when the door opens
and lets the future in."
Graham Greene, *The Power & The Glory*

PROLOGUE

SHORTLY AFTER 3PM on August 7th 1942, a Bristol Bombay transport plane took off from the desert airfield of Burg el Arab, the tented headquarters of the British Eighth Army in North Africa. It was heading across the desert to the Heliopolis military hospital on the banks of the Nile.

At the controls was "Jimmy" James, a nineteen-year-old pilot from a coal-mining village in South Wales. The summer heat of the Sahara had turned James's cockpit, a bubble of thin Perspex, into an oven. James was relieved to be airborne: his main concern at that moment was to get out of the battle zone as quickly as possible. For although the Bristol Bombay was held in considerable affection among the troops of the Eighth Army, who dubbed her the "mother duck" because she was the chief deliverer of the troops' mail, she was an antiquated plane that had been withdrawn from service in Europe, and her fixed undercarriage and slow speed made her an easy target for enemy fighters.

On that hot summer's day Jimmy James was making the journey back to the hospital later than usual. He had only arrived at the front line at about two thirty pm and had then been further delayed when, waiting on the runway for the mailsacks to be offloaded, and the wounded soldiers to be ferried onto the plane on their stretchers, he had suddenly been told to wait.

"Switch off your engines!" a voice had yelled at him from the hut. "There's an important passenger on his way you're to take with you."

Just then two staff cars pulled up. Out of one of them emerged "Strafer" Gott. James recognised the tall bear-like figure immediately; Gott was one of the most popular generals in the desert, a large, rugby-playing, former infantry battalion commander with a loud voice and pugnacious spirit. What James didn't know was that Churchill had just appointed him commander of the entire Eighth Army.

After being told of his promotion, Gott had asked Churchill for a few days of leave in Cairo before taking up his new command. Rather than demand his own plane, he had insisted on hitching a ride on the first troop carrier he could find.

"Are you the captain?" the General had asked James.

"Yes sir," replied the coalminer's son. "I'm terribly sorry, sir, I don't have a hat so I can't salute you."

"My boy, don't worry about that," Gott smiled. "Are you ready to go?"

"Yes, sir."

With relief, James had showed the General to his seat in the back among the stretchers swinging from the hooks in the ceiling, and apologised for the lack of space and comfort. Again, Gott reassured him: "Don't worry about me, I'll sit anywhere."

*

That August, Hitler and the Third Reich were invincible. In the space of three short years, all of Western Europe with the exception of Britain had fallen under their control, and it seemed only a matter of time before Britain too would be forced to bow before Berlin. Morale within the British army was very low.

Having been driven out of Europe at Dunkirk two years earlier, there was now only one place on earth that the British army was actually engaging German forces, and that was in the desert of North Africa.

Yet here, too, defeat piled upon defeat.

The German commander in North Africa, Erwin Rommel, and his Afrika Corps had attained an almost mythic status among German and British troops alike. In little more than seven months they had pushed the mighty British Empire back a thousand miles, from Tripoli through Libya and Egypt, right to the gates of Cairo. Beyond that lay Palestine and the rich oil fields of Iraq and Iran; if Germany could secure access to the oil of the Middle East it would have enough fuel to run its armies indefinitely and the Allies would be crippled.

Churchill was acutely embarrassed by the performance of his desert forces. Two months earlier, in June 1942, Rommel had captured the key city of Tobruk in a single day, taking 35,000 British soldiers prisoner. When the Germans then crossed into Egypt, the Middle East Command drew up plans to evacuate into Palestine. In the streets of Cairo, Egyptians jeered the British imperialists, chanting "Advance Rommel".

Desperate to prove to his American allies that Britain could stand up against the Germans, Churchill bombarded his generals with telegrams, ordering them to stop retreating and to go on the offensive. "Defeat is one thing: disgrace is another," he wrote despairingly in his diaries.

In an attempt to salvage the situation, General Claude Auchinleck, the commander of the Eighth Army, ordered a defensive line to be built at the tiny village of El Alamein; it was a well chosen spot with the sea on one flank and the vast salt marsh of the Qattarah Depression, which was impenetrable to all vehicles, on the other.

By August, Auchinleck had forced the Afrika Corps to a standstill. Rommel's huge advance had taken him far from his supplies and his troops were beginning to suffer; he lacked petrol for his tanks, and some days the German soldiers were having to survive in the desert heat on half a cup of water a day. The Germans still had the momentum, however, and among the British troops there was a mood of defeatism; Auchinleck was so in awe of Rommel's reputation that he banned all mention of his name around his headquarters.

Exasperated and impatient for results, Churchill flew out to Cairo on 3rd August 1942, intending to instil some backbone into the British forces. He was looking for a larger than life figure, someone with swagger and self-confidence, who believed he could beat Rommel and drive a dagger through the bogey of retreat. He settled on General William Gott.

*

Behind the perspex canopy in the "mother duck", James sweated even more than normal; he had never flown a VIP before. But he barely had time to focus on the implications. As he lifted off the desert floor, the temperature gauge showed that his engines were overheating. He needed to climb quickly up to the cooler air, but until he was out of enemy range he was forced to fly at 50 feet to avoid detection. The Bristol Bombay was not only flying alone, it was virtually unarmed. The Royal Air Force was so short of weapons that they had replaced the two Vickers guns in the tail turret with wooden dummies. Its normal complement of two gunners had been replaced by a single medical orderly.

James had been airborne only three or four minutes when two Messerschmitts appeared from behind. He heard a loud bang and looked out to see the starboard engine stuttering. Then came cannon tracers ripping through the wing. Flames sucked out of the engine, filling the cockpit with oily black smoke.

James began searching frantically for somewhere to land and at the same time yelling at the Second Pilot to get the Medical Orderly from the back. There was another bang and the propeller on the port side started to slow. The plane was now gliding without power. James pulled back the controls to gain as much height as he could while he still had speed.

He saw the pair of Messerschmitt 109s hurtle past once more; this time they punctured his main fuel tanks and fuel began pouring into the stricken aircraft between the cockpit and the passenger area. As he looked back he could see that his wireless operator had been badly injured in the arm.

"Get all the wounded off the stretcher hooks and lie them on the floor," James yelled.

Ahead, the desert sloped away in a long descent. James glided the plane down and with flying skill well beyond his years gently touched the front wheels onto the desert floor. But the crosswind held up the tail, preventing the rear wheels from landing. He dared not use his brakes in case the plane flipped.

Struggling to see through the smoke in the cockpit, he tried to swerve between the rocks strewn over the sand, kicking his rudders one way and then the other. It felt as if he was driving a ten-ton truck. He could see his charred hands on the control stick but the pain seemed far away. Slowly the tail came down; he began to apply the brakes. There was no response. The brake cables had been shot away. All he could do was to keep the plane upright and wait for the soft sand to slow the plane's momentum.

Gradually his speed dropped: 70, 60, 50 miles an hour. When the dial reached 40, James told the Second Pilot to warn the passengers to stand by to evacuate.

"Get the back door off and when I give the word drop them onto the sand."

Smoke choked his lungs. The Messerschmitts were returning for a third run.

"Stand by! Open the hatch on the cockpit floor," James yelled at the medical orderly. The "mother duck" hit a patch of soft sand and the speed dropped sharply. Peering back through the smoke James thought he saw someone in the back giving a thumbs up.

"Now!" he shouted.

The wireless operator, Medical Orderly and Second Pilot disappeared through the hatch in the floor and suddenly James was alone. Hoping he'd done everything he could, he slid off his seat and crawled towards the hole in the floor as cannon fire ripped open the Perspex canopy above his head.

The plane groaned to a halt and he sank onto the desert floor. He was surprised to find that, instead of making a six-foot fall, he hit the sand only a foot away – the Bombay's landing gear had finally buckled. It had bumped along the desert floor for over eight miles. He scrambled out of the smoke into the searing afternoon sun, expecting to find 20 people scattered behind, but there were just four: the wounded Wireless Operator, the Second Pilot, a wounded soldier and the Medical Orderly.

"The passengers – where are they?" he asked incredulously.

They pointed at the burning plane which was beginning to change shape, twisting and buckling in the heat.

"The rear door is jammed."

James stared at the door, watching as the camouflage paintwork blistered. Flames billowed furiously in the wind. When he tried to approach, he was blown back. The new commander of the Eighth Army was being incinerated.

Telling the Medical Orderly to look after the others, James set out across the desert to try to find help. His shoes and socks were burned, his shorts frayed, his shirt in shreds. He could see that one of his boots was full of blood. Alternating between walking and jogging, he covered about three miles, before passing out on top of a sand ridge.

Several hours later, passing Tuareg tribesmen spotted the figure. Picking him up, they laid him across one of their camels and brought him to a nearby Army post.

From there a rescue party was sent out, guided by the column of smoke on the horizon, but by the time they reached the plane, it was a charred shell.

News of Gott's death reached the Prime Minister as he was on his way to bed in the British Embassy in Cairo. One of his staff officers stopped him on the stairs.

"It may be a blessing in disguise," said the officer ,but Churchill scowled at him. It didn't feel like one. Those around Churchill had had deep reservations about Gott. The Chief of the Imperial General Staff (CIGS), General Alan Brooke, considered Gott exhausted and out of his depth, but Churchill had brushed aside Brooke's warning. Now however, he had run out of generals in the field; the Eighth Army had been through four commanders in nine months. Someone would have to be summoned from the Home Front.

Brooke urged Churchill to call up Lt-General Bernard Montgomery, who was was then in charge of the South-Eastern Army in southern England. As a young infantry captain during the First World War Montgomery had earned a reputation for leadership and bravery. He had won a DSO during the first Battle of Ypres. By the start of the Second World War, he was a junior general in charge of a division. At Dunkirk he had shown an ability to remain calm under the intense pressure of retreat when many, including his own superiors like John Gort, the head of the British Army, seemed paralysed by indecision. He had withdrawn his troops to the coast with minimal casualties and in the midst of the chaos he had been promoted to Commander of Second Corps.

Yet Montgomery wasn't considered one of Britain's "top drawer" generals. Ever since Dunkirk he had been passed over repeatedly for command in the field and had been languishing in Britain. Command of the South-Eastern Army was considered almost a Home Guard post. At the age of 55, many felt he had risen as far as he was going to go.

Churchill demurred at Brooke's suggestion. The Prime Minister regarded Montgomery as not completely "reliable", slightly unhinged even. Montgomery's obsession with training in peacetime had verged on zealotry and he had a reputation – even in an institution not known for its humility – for being arrogant in the extreme and sometimes vicious towards his peers. He did not hide his disdain of fellow officers and those superiors whom he considered "not up to the task". Montgomery clearly needed careful handling. Being so mercurial himself, Churchill preferred his generals to be more straightforward.

Churchill's first choice for the job was "Jumbo" Wilson, a solid unspectacular general then in command of the British forces in Syria and a personal favourite of the Prime Minister's. Churchill argued that he was a safe pair of hands with desert experience, whereas Montgomery was an enormous gamble for such a critical mission – he had never served in the Middle East and no one knew if he possessed the strategic vision to beat a general as gifted as Rommel. This was the last throw of the dice; if the next commander failed like all the others then the British would be pushed out of the Middle East completely.

Brooke persisted. He had studied Montgomery closely during those heart-stopping few days in Dunkirk and he believed that Montgomery had both a steeliness and a careful methodical approach to campaigning that had been lacking so far in the desert generals. He badgered his boss to put his personal antipathy about Monty's character to one side and to take a chance with him.

Shortly after midnight, Churchill finally relented. With some trepidation, he ordered a telegram to be sent to the War Office requiring Montgomery's services.

Montgomery received the phone call from the War Office as he was shaving the next morning at his house in Portsmouth. As far as he was concerned, he had spent his whole life preparing for just such an event. He knew immediately that he'd been handed an opportunity he would not get again; The unpleasant death of Gott –

a man ten years younger than him – was the pivotal moment which would turn the 55-year-old unknown Bernard Law Montgomery into "Monty": Field Marshal Montgomery of El Alamein and the most famous English general since Wellington. Soon Brooke was calling that crash in the desert an intervention by God.

1.

MY FATHER, RICHARD CARVER, was Monty's stepson. At the time of these events, he was a 28-year-old officer in the Royal Engineers, studying the art of war at the new British Army Staff College, at Haifa in Palestine. He greeted the news of Monty's promotion with mild surprise. Like everyone else, he assumed that Monty had already reached the top of his career. He would never have guessed the impact his stepfather was about to have on the course of the Second World War.

My father and Monty were very different characters. Through the power of his personality and his own iron conviction in himself, Monty asserted his authority over every room he entered. He had the quality of a flint stone; rough, angular, hard-headed and quick to spark. He was in perpetual impatient movement, probing, demanding, boasting, joking, harassing, criticising, raging. But his physical appearance, with his short stature and bristly nature, was more like that of a sergeant-major than a general.

My father, on the other hand, had been given all the looks and bearing of a military leader. Slightly over six foot, he towered over his stepfather. He had light blue eyes, well defined cheek bones and a strong jawline. His black hair was parted to one side and slicked down in the manner of an Allan Quartermain or Richard Hannay, or one of the other imaginary heroes of the books that my mother loved to read to me. But the appearance was deceptive, for he had none of Monty's braggadocio swagger and confidence; he possessed instead the slightly reserved manner of a country doctor.

*

When I was growing up in the 1960s I knew very little about my father. Like so many men of his generation, who had experienced the frequent prospect of dying, he kept his feelings hidden. Schooled to put duty to country before all else, he seemed to fear that too much emotion, like too much drink, might weaken his resolve. Talking about himself he considered boastful, even sinful. All I knew was that he had fought in the war and that he was now a teacher. This was not a profession that scored highly among English schoolboys, and so I barely mentioned him. And anyway I had Monty to brag about, a bona fide war hero, whom no one could compete with. As Monty's step-grandson, I did not carry his name but I still won the playground competition for who had the most famous relative.

At seven and a half, I was sent away to a prep school among the damp ferns and oaks of the Dorset countryside, called Dumpton. It was aptly named – a dumping-ground for the off-spring of army officers and colonial civil servants. There we played endless games of "Germans and English" in the bushes down by the cricket pitch, crawling through the undergrowth imagining we were part of some elite band of special forces. At night after lights out, we swapped Commando "trash mags" in our dormitories, reading them by torchlight under our covers.

Occasionally, Monty would send me, via my parents, stamps from his fan mail for my stamp collection. The stamps were always much bigger and more colourful than the drab British varieties and came from places like Paraguay and Madagascar that hovered at the very edges of my known world. The smaller and more insignificant the country the more impressive the stamps seemed to be. My friends and I would stare in wonder at the palm trees and the birds with vast wing-spans – a couple of the stamps had even managed to go halfway round the world without receiving a postmark, which my friend Garnett authoritatively said increased their value 100 times.

But it was the envelopes that attracted true awe: often the address said only "General Montgomery, somewhere near London, England", or "Field Marshal hero of El Alamein, British Isles". I would let my friends rub their grubby fingers reverently along the jagged slit of the envelopes, as they pictured the great general opening the letter over his morning toast and tea. Snotty, homesick, permanently hungry, our heads full of Latin gerunds and strange facts about county cricket, picked on by masters and older boys and with no possessions to our name except a tuck box and a few teddy bears, we could hardly conceive of anyone being so famous.

By the time I was nine or ten and old enough to remember him, Monty had disappeared from public life and was living in solitary retirement in Hampshire with his housekeeper and cook, surrounded by mementos of his battles – his wife Betty, Richard's mother, my grandmother, having died suddenly in 1938.

After the war ended, Monty had hoped that a grateful nation would give him some kind of reward for his services – after all, Queen Anne had once built Blenheim Palace for the Duke of Marlborough as a prize for a much more insignificant military campaign. In September 1945 he had appealed to the King's Private Secretary, declaring, "I have nowhere which my stepsons and my own boy can come to and call 'home'." He had lost nearly all his possessions when an incendiary bomb destroyed the Portsmouth warehouse in which they were stored, and the only accommodation he owned were two campaign caravans that he had lived in for three years, from El Alamein to Germany.

His appeal was rejected, however, by a post-war government, which was both bankrupted and conscious of people's fatigue. And so, grumbling about the miserly ingrates of Whitehall, Monty bought a dilapidated watermill and a skirt of boggy water meadows called Isington Mill on the River Wey. It was the first house he had ever owned. With his usual discipline, he assembled an army of gardeners who turned the ancient unkempt meadows into a huge lawn where every blade was cut to regulation height and no mole was allowed to raise its dusty head.

On Sunday exeats, my parents would pick me up from Dumpton and drive down to Isington Mill for Sunday lunch. Despite the lustre of fame that Monty's achievements brought to our otherwise unremarkable family, I think my mother would have preferred a warmer, jollier type of grandfather for her children; but, since both of our natural grandfathers were dead, Monty was all we had.

His mystique no longer held much sway for my five older teenage brothers and sisters; they resented the way he ordered them around as if they were his soldiers and did all they could to get out of the Sunday visits. So usually it was just my parents and I who went to see him. I would spend two hours rolling around the back of our delapidated Morris Minor, trying to read my Tintin books. Standing on his gravel drive, my father would prep me as my mother flattened down my hair and straightened me out.

"What are you going to say if he asks you?"

"That I want to be a soldier?"

"Good," my father would say, reaching for the door bell.

As a boy, I was deeply impressed by the power Monty had once wielded. I used to stare slackjawed at the black and white newsreels of the D-Day landings, which showed beaches teeming with landing craft, tanks, trucks, earth movers and hundreds of thousands of tiny figures sweating through the surf with their helmets and their backpacks. Above them the sky was congested

Top: Isington Mill, the house in Hampshire that Monty bought after the war. Below: Monty outside one of the caravans, in which he lived for much of the war, and which he later installed in a shed in his garden

Courtesy of Douglas Glass

with anti-barrage balloons and the puffs of the ack-ack. Then the scene would change and a small foxy-looking figure would appear, standing in some field with Churchill or hopping down from an aeroplane to greet Eisenhower. And the old-fashioned voice of the British Movietone News commentator would intone, "General Montgomery, the hero of El Alamein, has been summoned by Churchill to lead our invasion of Europe and to end this war once and for all..."

It was hard to connect this semi-mythic figure to the elderly person I would greet in the hallway, and yet he was unmistakably the same man. There were the same sharp features and the brisk, classless voice, incapable of any modulation below the imperative. At 80 years old, he still longed to be the focus of the world's attention, and lunches would often consist of Monty boasting of how much better he would run the country than the imbeciles that were currently in charge.

One particular Sunday lunch I sat in the kitchen of Isington Mill watching Monty's cook preparing the roast beef listening with one ear to her complaints to the maid about Monty's stinginess and with the other to the conversation coming through the open door of the dining room where lunch was in progress. Around the table were several rather forbidding-looking generals who had served under him in one or other of his campaigns and their wives, along with my parents.

I tried to follow the conversation, hoping for some nugget that I could take back to school and retell to my dormitory after lights out. The generals with their perfectly laundered white handkerchiefs and their dress medals glittering on their jackets, seemed terrifyingly formal and grand – although one of them, I noticed, had a speck of paper tissue on his cheek where he must have nicked himself shaving. As I stared at him through the open door, I realised Monty was telling a story about his time as a young subaltern in the First World War.

"The first occasion I was ordered to go 'over the top', I rushed up the side of the parapet and immediately tripped over my sword scabbard," Monty said with a dry laugh. "By the time, I'd picked myself up and rushed forward again, half of my troop had been killed." He then described how he had crawled into No Man's Land to try to observe the enemy positions. It took only ten minutes for a sniper hiding in a tree to spot him.

"His first bullet went through my right lung and produced a large amount of blood," he said. One of his soldiers, he explained, crawled forward to help. As the soldier tried to plug the hole in Monty's chest with a field dressing, the sniper put a bullet through his head. The man's body fell on top of Monty, pushing him down into the mud.

"The sniper kept firing at me. I got one more bullet in the left knee, but most of them hit the soldier. It was the dead man who saved my life," he said to the table.

Enthralled by the story, I hadn't noticed the maid nudging me. She was carrying ten small bone china cups on a silver tray. "You going to hand round the chocolates or not?"

It was my moment; I had been given the role of passing round the box of Black Magic with the coffee. I walked into the room behind the maid holding the black box out in front of me like the king's sceptre. I went to Monty's chair first. He grabbed me round the shoulders in his bony embrace.

"Dick's son," he stated.

Monty had an odd way of leaving out some words as if they were a waste of time. "Young Tom." He avoided calling me his grandson because of course, strictly speaking, we were not blood relations. There were nods of approval from the grey-haired men.

"Finest men I ever fought with," he said, waving his free hand in a sweep of benediction around the room and receiving back several indulgent smiles for me. I was then pushed off to circumnavigate the table, watched by the generals and their wives. Somehow in my nervousness, when I was about halfway round, the box came out of my hands and crashed to the floor.

I quickly sank under the table and scrabbled among the sharp trouser edges in search of errant walnut whirls and cream fudges. Shoes flicked in irritation as I stretched across them. I felt relieved to be under here in the strange forest of table legs and dark trousers where no one could see my burning cheeks. One long face peered under the table cloth to see what was going on and chuckled with amusement.

Then: "Get out boy!" came the rasping voice. "Leave that to the staff and go outside. Find something to play with in the garden."

It had been raining. There were two hours left before I had to be back at Dumpton for evensong. A cloud of gloom descended, knowing that I would not be with my parents tonight but in Dutton dormitory.

A shed stood at the far end of the garden. It was made of brand new pine and looked slightly out of place amid the wet greenery. I pushed at the doors. In the weak autumn light, I could make out two small caravans nose to tail squeezed under the roof as if the barn had been built around them. One was a desert brown, the other battlefield green. I opened the door of the first. It was the size of a yacht's cabin and smelt of the military, that hollow aroma of brass cleaner, dampness, leather and sweat. I walked gingerly around, slowly inspecting everything in turn. One end was taken up by a bed, a sink and a toilet. The bed was neatly made with blankets and a pillow as if ready to be mobilised one final time. A single picture hung on the wall. It was a portrait of an aristocratic-looking man in German uniform. Around his neck I noticed he wore the Iron Cross. I recognised him as Rommel, the "Desert Fox", Monty's greatest adversary.

A large folding desk stood open in the middle of the room. On the wall above the desk was a map covered in some kind of plastic sheeting which in turn was covered in dozens of lines and unfamiliar symbols. Half the lines were in green and half in red; some of them were unimpeded, others stopped

25

suddenly, confronted by squares and thick Xs. I had read enough Commando mags to know that these were battle-lines.

I lay down on the bed and imagined that the wind outside was the scream of Messerschmitts dive-bombing overhead. I stared at the map, trying to interpret the strange hieroglyphics. Night after night Monty must have lain in this same bed under the desert moon worrying about what Rommel was going to do next. I looked again at the picture, the German general was half smiling, and seemed to me to have quite a kind face.

I wondered where my father had been in all this. I knew that he had reached the rank of colonel, for that was how all the letters that arrived at home were addressed, to Colonel ROH Carver OBE. But what had he done? Had he ever been to any of the strange names that I could see on the map: El Alamein, Mersa Matruh, Burg-el-Arab, Fuka? Had he been part of that long green line of advance which snaked along the length of North Africa from Cairo to Tunis? The only tangible evidence that he had fought in the war was a deep indentation a few inches above his right ankle which he said had come from a piece of shrapnel that had gone in one side of his leg and come out the other. My mother had once told me that he had escaped from a POW camp and lived in "a cave".

As I willed the elusive markings on the map to come to life, I could hear my parents calling me back to the Mill. On an impulse, I decided to add some of my own. Since the greens appeared to be winning, I joined in on their side. I found a green chinagraph in the desk and drew a few more lines on Monty's battle plan, but instead of following the others I pushed them out into the blue of the Mediterranean far away from the shore.

*

It wasn't until many years later, when he was retired and I was grown up, that my father showed a greater willingness to talk about his past. As I learned what he had done, and the extraordinary

**The portrait of Rommel, by Wolfgang Willrich, which Monty
hung on the wall of his caravan**

adventures he had had, I began urging him to write down his experiences. I pointed out that the books that Monty had written about
the war – *The Path to Leadership, Normandy to the Baltic, El Alamein to
the River Sangro* – barely mentioned my father's story. These were
books full of battle orders, artillery plans, and lessons on how to
fight a combined air and land war, all intended to nail Monty's
own place in history. And the many books, written by others about
Monty, made no reference to my father either.

Finally, one winter in the late 1980s, my father gave in to my
entreaties, retired to his study and worked away. As the first prim-
roses and daffodils appeared in his garden below his study window,
he announced that he had finished. The result was characteristically short, just twenty pages long. It was entitled "Behind the lines
in Italy, a Personal Account of my time as a Prisoner of War in
1942/43". He called it his "pamphlet".

We got 200 copies printed privately and sent them around the
extended family. My father was moved by the enthusiastic respons-

es he received back from grandchildren and cousins. And yet, far from being a full rendering of what had happened, the pamphlet only hinted at further things unknown. It was a bloodless rendering of events and the hardships he'd endured. Like the campaign lines on the maps in the caravan, it concealed more than it revealed.

Then one weekend, in the 1990s, while clearing out a shelf in his house I came across an old metal cigarette case. The cigarette manufacturer's markings had been rubbed away, and smoothed by repeated handling, returning the tin to its original dark metallic brown. I opened it carefully as it looked as if the hinges were about to disintegrate.

The tin contained a small black bakelite cap about an inch and a half wide, over the top of which someone had attached a roughly cut piece of Perspex with sticking-plaster. Through the Perspex I could see a safety pin bent into the shape of an arrow and pushed down over what looked like a small brass coat button. As I turned the cap around trying to understand it, the safety pin suddenly came to life and began to move; I could see that it was not stuck down but floating on top of a second even smaller upright pin. Underneath it, written on a piece of cardboard inside the cap were the letters N, S, E and W. It was a homemade compass which I realised my father must have used to guide his way home through enemy lines.

In the bottom of the tin was a piece of carefully folded paper greyed by fingering. A map, or at least a copy of a map of what looked like a part of Italy.

When I showed my father my discoveries, he rummaged around in a box under his desk and pulled out a small notebook, bound in dark green leather and no bigger than a packet of cigarettes. Like the tin, the leather was as smooth as glass to touch, and stained. I opened the cover slowly, fearful that the desiccated binding might snap in half. The pages, still faintly lined, pulled apart reluctantly; each one was covered in a diminutive pencil handwriting, the words crammed tightly together. Some of the pages were heavily smudged; others appeared to be written in a kind of a code. This was his diary, my father explained, that he had kept during the summer and winter of 1943 while he was on the run.

A compass. A map. A diary. The lodestones of my father's war. The tantalising keynotes of a story still only haltingly told...

2.

IN 1970, my father took me to see the Hollywood film Patton. My father never took any of us to the cinema – he considered places of public gatherings like cinemas and pubs to be slightly dissolute and "inappropriate" – but he decided that I needed to see Patton. I was nine years old. The American general had been Monty's greatest rival in the Second World War; their arguments and antipathy for each other were legendary.

Being an American production, George Patton was portrayed in the film as a flawed but towering genius, whereas Monty came across as an English buffoon. He was played by a British comedy actor called Michael Bates who later starred in such classics as *No Sex Please We're British*, *It Ain't Half Hot Mum* and *Kamikaze in a Coffee Bath*. I sat on the creaking seats in Fleet Odeon, their red velour pockmarked with cigarette burns, staring up at the Stukas flying over the hot dusty souks, the American soldiers jumping in and out of their jeeps and Patton striding among the ruins of Carthage.

I was mesmerised by the vast canvas of war, but beside me

my father took each appearance by Monty in the film as a personal offence.

"That's ridiculous", he muttered, "Monty wasn't like that at all."

He grumbled softly at first, then louder and louder until people began to turn around in their seats. As Patton was leaving Italy and heading for the green cornfields of Northern Europe and D Day, my father decided we'd all seen enough and I found myself being pushed past people out of the cinema and back onto the rainy high street.

"What a lot of rubbish," he said in disgust.

His anger was all the more startling because my father so rarely displayed any strong emotion, especially in public. I was bewildered at the time, annoyed not to be allowed to see the film through to the end. But, with hindsight, I can see why he found the caricatural portrayal of Monty so upsetting. Monty may have been prickly and difficult, but he was the only father figure that my father had.

*

In January 1926, my grandmother Betty Carver arrived for a winter holiday at Lenk in Switzerland with her two sons, Richard, my father, aged 11, and his brother John, who was two years older. Their father, Oswald, had died a decade earlier, hit at close range by Turkish machine guns while leading his men across the scrubby fields above Gallipoli.

In the years that had followed, the memory of Oswald became sacred to Betty. The photos of him show a tall athletic figure with dark good looks. He had attended Trinity Cambridge and won a blue rowing for the university. The following year he had rowed for Britain in the 1908 London Olympics in front of a huge home crowd. He was well off, handsome and mildly heroic.

Oswald's family, the Carvers, were serious-minded "chapel

folk" who, in the space of a generation, had managed to rise up from carting goods over the Pennines to become substantial cotton traders and manufacturers. They were the biggest employer in the small town of Marple outside Manchester with 300 people clocking in to the Carver cotton mill for work every morning. The 1911 census showed that the Carver household employed seven servants and three grooms for their horses at their large estate, Cranage Hall.

All that changed with the First World War. Oswald and his brother never returned. Then the Great Depression sent the price of English cotton plummeting and in 1927 the family was forced to sell the mill and Cranage Hall. The only bidder was the local authority which turned the large Victorian mansion into a lunatic asylum. The walls were whitewashed in lime, the carpets taken up the boards scrubbed with disinfectant and soon the long corridors were filled with the mumblings of the insane, heard only by the cows grazing in the pasture outside. The Carvers' brief membership of the leisured classes had expired before it had really begun.

Richard and John moved with their widowed mother to a small cottage on the banks of the Thames in Chiswick. If they occasionally missed not having a father, they were far from alone in their situation among boys of their age and they enjoyed the full attention of their mother. Betty Carver was warm and vivacious, an aspiring painter. The cottage was full of her friends, nearly all poets and artists. In the evenings Richard and John lay upstairs in their beds listening to the noise of conversation below.

That winter of 1926, they had something to celebrate: at the encouragement of Augustus John, Betty Carver had applied to the Slade School of Art and to her delight and due no doubt to a word of recommendation from him, she had been accepted. She decided to raid the small trust fund that her in-laws had set aside for Richard and John's education and take them on a winter holiday.

The Hotel Wildstrubel was not Lenk's most fashionable hotel but not its worst either. On the second morning there, Betty and the two boys were having breakfast in the dining room when an Englishman walked up to their table and introduced himself. He had a neatly clipped moustache and was dressed for some reason in lederhosen, as if trying to fit in with the local scene. He was short, with vivid blue eyes and a beaky nose. When he spoke it was with a wiry nervous energy as if he didn't have time to explain his thoughts in great detail. The image that came to Richard's mind was of a Jack Russell dog.

In what seemed to be a single breath, the man explained that he had been recently promoted as a major in the British infantry and was holidaying alone in Lenk. He said that he had been drawn to their breakfast table by the presence of children, having none of his own. He appeared to be nearing forty and a confirmed bachelor with no sign of a wife. In fact, though he didn't reveal it to Betty, he had come to Lenk in pursuit of a girl he had developed an infatuation with the summer before, but the girl, who was much younger, had firmly rebuffed him.

In her casual and slightly detached way, Betty invited the major to spend the day with them. Richard and John enjoyed the presence of this man who was the same age as their father would have been had he lived. Despite being an indifferent skier, this eccentric officer had no shortage of theories about how it should be done; in a parent this might have been grating but Richard and John were attracted by his energy and enthusiasm. He was always willing to join in with whatever they were doing; they laughed each time he fell over – there was something comical about the way he would bounce straight back up, shaking the snow off himself as if trying to pretend that he had never fallen. He was an amusing companion and when the holiday ended, they said all said friendly goodbyes.

The next year the three of them returned once more to Lenk. In the interim they had not thought much more about the major, and so the boys were surprised to see him striding towards them across the lobby of the hotel on the first day as if he had never left. They were even more struck by Betty's greeting. They noticed that she did not seem at all surprised by the coincidence of the meeting – as if she had been expecting to find him here. This time the Major did not confine his opinions to the ski slope. He was clearly used to giving orders and having them obeyed.

"You must discipline in the home," they heard him say to her one day with what they considered excessive familiarity, but Betty only smiled and ignored the questioning glances that the boys threw in her direction.

Three months after they returned from skiing in the Easter holidays of 1927, Betty took Richard to visit his new school, Charterhouse. John was already there and had filled Richard with alarming stories about the fierce regime, the cold baths every morning, and having to wear the "attire of a city gent" with a jacket and pinstripes and a bowler hat. Adding to Richard's confusion and distress, the major from Lenk – now a colonel and dressed in a crisp staff officer's uniform – turned up unexpectedly at Betty's side.

The school echoed with memories of the Great War. As they walked down the long shining corridors that smelt of beeswax, Richard stared up at the walls that held the names of the seven hundred Carthusians who had fallen in the fields of northern France; the great battles – Ypres, Flanders and Passchendaele - were inscribed in gold lettering as if they had been fought by gods. They toured the school's new chapel designed by the famous architect Sir Gilbert Scott which had been opened that year as a memorial to the fallen. In one of the rooms, John showed his younger brother the 3 VCs won by Charterhouse boys displayed proudly under glass.

Just then Colonel Montgomery announced that he wanted to "inspect" the sports facilities – he seemed to assume that everything was there for his benefit – so John, too awed to protest, led them solemnly around the tennis courts and then the fives and racquets building. My father remembered his metal heel caps echoing on the parquet flooring.

Inside one of the fives courts the colonel halted. Betty told John to take Richard away for a few minutes so that she and the colonel could be alone. Bewildered and with the impending nausea of homesickness in his stomach, Richard let John lead him up the stairs to the spectators' gallery. They pretended to play together, but they couldn't take their eyes off the two figures standing in the middle of the court talking in subdued tones.

"It'll be alright," said John jocularly, punching Richard's arm, but both knew it would not be. Richard sensed that this man was about to disturb their cosy family triangle. After a few moments, Betty looked up, smiled and waved at the boys, beckoning them back. Richard raced down, hurrying to stand next to her to shut out the bristly little figure on the other side.

"Bernard and I are going to get married," she said. At first, Richard did not hear what she had said, preoccupied with his own thoughts. Then seeing the astonished expression on John's face, he asked her to repeat the news.

"We're getting married," Monty interjected.

*

The match was greeted with horror by Betty's circle of friends. Betty introduced him into her artistic salons and Monty sat in the small living room of the cottage gamely trying to contribute something to the conversations about Art Deco and Futurism, but the only thing he liked to talk about was the art of war, a subject he could expound on with great passion for hours. Betty's friends concluded that he was an eccentric in the wrong mould, obsessed by what had gone wrong in the First World War, which none of them wanted to think about. It was too dull and depressing. They feared that his fierce sense of discipline and routine would overwhelm Betty's fragile sensibilities. He's a philistine who has never read

35

a thing, they told each other.

But to everyone's surprise, Betty didn't seem to care about the difference in their temperaments. Though she had no interest in her fiancé's military world, she was attracted by his passion; the way he became so excited and voluble over strange issues like the role of the tank in future warfare and the benefits of enfilade fire. She detected within him a surfeit of raw emotional energy. During that period of the 1920s, when the rest of the world had had their fill of war, Monty could not stop talking about it. He seemed to be planning for some new conflict in the future that Betty had no concept of. Besides, she was tired of being the only parent and she wanted to be looked after. And she certainly felt loved by this strange, compelling man.

On June 25th 1927, an announcement appeared in the *Times* of an engagement between Lt. Colonel Bernard Montgomery and Mrs E.A. Carver. They married quietly one month later; Monty insisting on having not one but two honeymoons, first in England and then in Switzerland.

Brushing aside the concerns of others, he immediately assumed the role of both husband and parent, oblivious to the fact that he had no experience of either. Monty couldn't bear to see anything that wasn't well run, and the only way he knew how to run anything was on military lines. He took over the management of the household chores and divided Betty's disorderly life into carefully allotted spans, posting "orders of the day" on the dining room door with instructions such as "lunch at 1300 hours" and "girls will pick up flowers for the house". Betty often ignored them but she nonetheless found the routine reassuring. She sold the old motorbike and sidecar that she used to drive her two boys around in, and allowed Monty to drive her in his stately Belsize. He took the two boys riding through the woods of Sandhurst and swimming in the lakes and thus, through the force of his character, he pulled all three of them into his gravitational field.

Betty understood that Monty's obsessive orderliness and self-discipline was a way of containing his inner demons. Monty had spent the early years of his life on the remote island of Tasmania off Australia, where his father had been an Anglican bishop, ministering to a parish largely populated by recidivist convicts.

For six months a year, the Bishop walked the hills of Tasmania in a bush hat and hobnail boots visiting the distant prison farms, while Maud, his much younger wife, ruled the home and their six children with a fierceness that bordered on cruelty. When Monty sold the bike that he had been given for his tenth birthday, she forced him to buy it back with every penny of his pocket money. The beatings were unrelenting: it was said that Maud Montgomery handled a cane like a man. But she was unable to bend the fifth of her six children to her will. On one occasion when Maud was trying to make herself heard at a children's party, Monty jumped on a table and yelled, "silence in the pig market, the old sow speaks first!"

The old Bishop, hoping that boarding school might temper his son's volcanic energy, sent him to St Paul's. But the 1906 school magazine gives a portrait of a boy unbowed, its sport section recorded Monty's demonic fury towards opposing teams in rugby: "stamping on their heads and twisting their necks and doing many other inconceivable atrocities with a view no doubt to proving his patriotism".

He decided to join the army largely to spite his parents who tried hard to push him into the church, and his military career was nearly derailed almost immediately when he set fire to the shirttails of a fellow cadet at the Royal Military Academy Sandhurst, badly burning him. Slowly, the military discipline and routine began to have some effect and Monty learnt to channel his energy into hard work. He fought through the First World War and emerged on the other side – minus part of a knee and a lung from snipers' bullets.

A year after his marriage to Betty, she gave him a son, David – the only child they had between them. In 1928, he took his new stepsons back to Lenk, this time without Betty. The three of them shared a room to economise. My father remembered Monty telling them how to pee.

"You boys are very uncivilised," he said, "you must stand up to use a chamber pot, not kneel down."

Brought up without a father, no one had told them. Monty kept reminding them "to keep to their partums". Each day was planned meticulously in advance, though the boys could not help noticing that it rarely went according to plan. Richard was surprised to discover that Monty had a keen sense of the absurd. They fooled around, having snowball fights and laughing at the outfits of some of the other guests. To the end of his life, my father remembered a limerick that Monty taught him on that holiday:

> *There was an old soldier from Lyme*
> *Who married 3 wives at a time*
> *When asked why the third*
> *He said, one's absurd*
> *And bigamy, sir, is a crime*

On the surface my father put on a brave face. When adults told him that he must be pleased to have a new father, he did not demur. He told his mother he was happy for her. But inside he was in mourning. Monty's arrival had severed the intimacy of the life that he and John had had with their mother in the cottage in Chiswick. They no longer had her full attention. She was now an army wife – a role for which she had sacrificed her dreams of being an artist – and at Christmas 1931, when Monty and his regiment were posted to Jerusalem, Betty left with him. From Palestine they would move onto Quetta on the Northwest Frontier, taking David, their three-year-old, with them and leaving behind John and Richard at boarding school.

Richard was by now in his late teens, and thinking about his future. Without Monty in his life, my father might have pursued

Betty with her boys: Richard and John (left and right, respectively), and David, the son she had by Monty

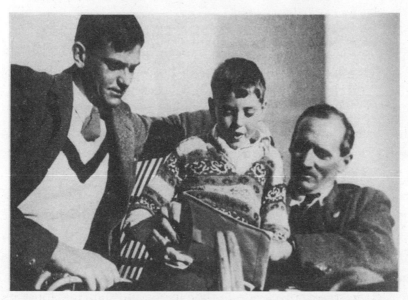

Richard (left), with Monty and David, 1936

a very different path, far away from the military. His own father Oswald had joined the army only because of the war; he had no intention of making it his career. And Betty had little to do with the military after he died. But, as Monty pushed and elbowed his way up through the cobwebbed ranks of Britain's imperial army, he dragged everyone along in his slipstream. After graduating from Cambridge, in 1936, Richard declared an interest in becoming an architect, but Monty persuaded him otherwise.

Monty and Betty, with her son Richard, and their son David, 1935

"We will fight Germany again before long," Monty said. "It's unavoidable."

He reminded Richard how Oswald his natural father had given his life fighting for his country. Richard did not resist and joined the Royal Engineers, Oswald's old corps; there was a part of him that wanted to win the respect of his stepfather.

*

In the summer of 1937, Monty was promoted to the rank of brigadier and acquired large army quarters in Portsmouth which Betty was delighted with. By then they had been married ten years; she had proved her friends wrong. She had found happiness with a man that most others found intolerable. Her gentleness had softened his nature if not his will, keeping him within the bounds of normal society.

Monty set about training his new brigade at once. Time was running out; he was convinced that England would soon be fighting Hitler and he wanted to be ready. Throughout the hot August of that year when many of his fellow officers were on the beaches or the grouse moors, he led his grumbling troops through manoeuvre after manoeuvre around Stonehenge and Cranborne Chase.

During summer troop manoeuvres there was an unspoken agreement that the working day would finish around five o'clock, in time for officers to catch the train up to London or travel to the pleasures of Bournemouth, but Monty wasn't interested. He made his brigade sleep in tents on different parts of Salisbury Plain and forced them through complex night movements in which they had to capture an opponent's position before dawn.

On August 21st, Betty took ten-year-old David for a beach holiday in Burnham-on-Sea, so that they could be near Monty on manoeuvres. The first day that Betty was on the beach, she was bitten by an insect. She was never able to tell the doctors what it was, but that night her leg began to swell and she was taken to the local cottage hospital. Monty came to see her. Assured by the doctors that it was only an inflammation from which she would recover, he left shortly afterwards.

As August moved into September, the infection spread throughout Betty's body. Antibiotics did not yet exist. Reluctant to interrupt his war-gaming, Monty visited her only briefly, always hurrying back to his brigade. For several weeks David played alone on the beach during the day, spending the evenings by his mother's bedside watching her steadily decline. By September, Monty could see that it was serious but felt there was little he could do; when term began he insisted that David return to his boarding school instead of staying by his mother's side.

"Perhaps I did wrong," he wrote later in a rare admission of error, "but I did what I thought was right."

Had she been strong enough to protest, Betty would surely have asked for David to remain, but by now she was slipping in and out of consciousness. The maid packed away David's beach clothes and filled his trunk with clothes for school. He was brought to the hospital to say goodbye. He bought her a little gold brooch in the shape of a sword as a parting present and stood by the side of the bed holding it, watching Betty toss from one side to the other, hoping that the fever might lift enough for her to notice him and say goodbye. But the time came for him to leave and she was still delirious. David laid the brooch softly down on her bedclothes beside her hand and left. Back at the hotel he wrote his mother a final note before he was driven to school. He seemed to be the only one who could see she was dying.

Betty lingered on for a few more weeks, but the doctors had run out of ideas. The poison from the bite, if that was the cause in the first place, had long since entered her bloodstream and taken over her entire body. In October, they decided on the amputation of her legs. It was a gesture of despair and she died in Monty's arms on October 19th. The post mortem recorded septicaemia. Later that day, sitting beside her bed, Monty wrote to Richard who was in India.

I found the letter many years later among my father's papers, written in Monty's thick-nibbed handwriting and carefully preserved by my father in its original envelope: "I think she knew she could not live. This morning when the doctor had left the room she whispered to me to go after him and ask him what he thought. And later when he came in again she gasped, 'Is there any hope?' Poor darling – she had a ghastly time during the last six weeks and had fought most bravely to live. I used to tell her she must fight for our sakes. But it was too much for her... Life is very black at the moment. I do not know what I shall do without her. It will be very hard for you to bear, away in India by yourself. Mummy looks very peaceful now. There is a look of complete calm and rest on her face."

*

Monty did not allow anyone from the family, even David, to attend her funeral. A single photo is all that remains of that day; it shows Monty walking back to his staff car from the graveside. He carries the air of a ghost, gaunt and withdrawn as if his soul had been ripped out. He returned to the empty house in Portsmouth and shut the door. "The funeral is over," he wrote on 21st October 1937. "I sat in the room at the hospital until they came to screw the lid on the coffin. I kissed her dear face for the last time just before the lid was put on. I tried hard to bear up at the service and at the graveside. But I could not bear it and I am afraid I broke down utterly. I feel desperately lonely and sad. I suppose in time I shall get over it, but at present it seems that I never shall."

For four days Monty refused to see anyone. Betty's death had caught him completely off guard. The man who prepared for every eventuality so meticulously had not foreseen the biggest tragedy of his life, though he'd had plenty of warning. Betty was the only person who ever loved him unreservedly, giving him love that had been denied by the cruel Maud. She didn't find his eccentricities exasperating, she charmed his superiors and tempered his overbearing manner by teasing, she brought laughter into his khaki world and stopped his obsessive tendencies from veering into something more extreme. And now she was gone.

Then one morning at 1am he called his brigade-major and

Burnham - on - Sea
19 - 10 - 37

My dear Dickie
        Our darling Mummie has been
taken from us. She developed bronchial
pneumonia on 14 October, and then
the poison in her system got into the
blood stream and finally into her
heart. I never left her for the last
24 hours and it was heart breaking

told him to have all his papers on his desk at 9am. From that moment on, he sunk himself into his work. Without Betty there were to be no more distractions in his life.

By the time he received Monty's letter, Richard already knew that his mother was dead. A telegram had found Richard two weeks earlier, in the officer's mess in Bangalore where he was living, stating simply, "Mummy died peacefully today. Pneumonia. Monty."

How shall I live without my
darling Betty. I do hope you
will be able to come home Dickie
in the Spring; I want to go
with you to visit her grave again.
        Monty

Extracts from Monty's letter to Richard, October 1937

3.

THE WEEKS THAT followed Gott's plane crash in the desert were a time of extreme pressure for Monty. As the fifth general in charge of the Eighth Army, everyone was looking to him to somehow staunch the haemorrhaging of defeat. Churchill badgered him to go on the offensive as fast as possible against Rommel. The Chief of the Imperial General Staff, General Alan Brooke, and the entire British military establishment appeared to be holding their breath, waiting for something to happen. But Monty was capable of extraordinary stubbornness. He would not be rushed, even by the Prime Minister.

He found himself in command of a strange stew of British, Australians, New Zealanders and Indian forces. At the first meeting with his senior staff on 13th August 1942, he declared:

"I have ordered that all plans and instructions dealing with further withdrawal are to be burnt, and at once. We will stand and fight here. If we can't stay here alive, then let us stay here dead... I have little more to say just at present. And some of you may think it is quite enough and may wonder if I am mad."

He paused and studied the 60 officers standing in front of him in the desert evening light.

"…I assure you I am quite sane. I understand there are people who often think I am slightly mad; so often that I now regard it as rather a compliment. All I have to say is that if I am slightly mad, there are a large number of people I could name who are raving lunatics!"

He scorned the rigid dress codes of the Army Handbook; he rarely wore a tie or badge of rank. Sometimes he would turn up in an Australian bushwhacker's broad rimmed hat, at other times he wore a beret with two cap badges on it instead of the regulation one. He was both disliked and admired by his peers in the army. He had no interest in belonging to any of their clubs or in playing polo, the game of British army officers; he neither drank nor smoked and made no attempt to endear himself in the officer's mess.

He was most at home with soldiers, easily overcoming the class barrier that separated most British generals from other ranks. He was a natural showman and was always happy to jump on the bonnet of a jeep and explain to a group of soldiers how he was going to knock Rommel 'out of Africa'.

When Churchill visited Monty a few days after he had taken up his command he found his habits quite baffling. They toured the Eighth Army's positions and stopped to have lunch with one of Monty's junior commanders. While Churchill and the commander dug into a three course lunch with wine, Monty insisted on staying in his car where he ate some sandwiches that had been prepared for him by his batman and drank lemonade from a flask. When Churchill asked him afterwards why he'd refused to join them, Monty explained that he never accepted hospitality from a subordinate commander on principle.

Churchill wondered if his eccentricities might be verging on the insane, but in time he came to see the value of having a general who cared little for how the world viewed him. If he is disagreeable to those about him, he commented, imagine how much more disagreeable he is to the enemy.

North Africa was a unique theatre of war. In Europe, the densely populated cities and fermenting ideologies had produced a potential inferno of personal animosities. Out in North Africa, however, the desert was flat, even and empty like a giant playing-field so that each battle felt not unlike a professional sports match; a trial of military strength unconfused by the warp of politics. The German commander, Erwin Rommel, was a professional soldier who was interested in winning battles but not in propagating Nazism. Even on the coast where the fighting occurred there were barely any towns or civilians. The only non-combatants that most soldiers ever saw were the occasional band of Tuareg tribesmen who continued to criss-cross the Sahara on their camel trains unaware of the existence of Adolf Hitler or a World War.

Each night soldiers from opposing armies would lie on their backs separated by only a few miles and stare up at the same field of stars that stretched uninterrupted from horizon to horizon, listening to the silence. "Lily Marlene", the German song, became popular with the British soldiers after they heard it being played by their German counterparts. Everyone felt the presence of the vast emptiness of sand.

In this world where all there was to do was to prepare and fight battles, Monty could not have been happier. Like Rommel, Monty was uninterested in politics; soldiering was a vocation to him. In his caravan on the beach at Burg-el-Arab he pinned the picture of Rommel by Willrich above his desk and studied his enemy. The painting – the same one that I stared at 25 years later – shows Rommel dressed in a greatcoat of grey. Tank goggles are pushed back on his head and the Iron Cross hangs around his neck. His expression betrays no hostility – it is the direct stare of the desert fox, determined to survive.

*

Rommel had no intention of allowing his new opponent time to settle in. On 31st August, eighteen days after Monty had arrived in the desert, Rommel unleashed his Panzer Divisions on a long sweep around the thinly-protected British southern flank. His plan was to lure the British out of their positions and force them to fight the kind of fast, mobile battle which the Deutsche Afrika Korps excelled at. Once they'd won, he would drive north towards the sea, cutting off the Eighth Army from its supplies and the road to Cairo would be his.

Auchinleck, Monty's predecessor, had anticipated this possibility and had ordered deep mine fields to be laid in the south. Just before the attack, the Ultra code breakers picked up Rommel's intentions and Monty hurriedly reinforced the high ridge on his southern flank known as Alam El Halfa with anti-tank guns, artillery and any spare Grant tanks that he could find. To lure Rommel's forces within range of his guns, he intentionally left a gap in the minefields below the ridgeline.

Rommel launched the attack under a full moon. The minefields slowed the advance and soon the German and Italian troops became bogged down. Eventually he gave up trying to break through and wheeled his panzer divisions around to attack the positions on the ridge. He had to get the British off the ridge and into the open. But Monty was waiting for them. The codebreakers in England had given Monty the time he needed to prepare. The German armoured vehicles were picked off by the British anti-tank guns and the RAF desert air force.

On 3rd September, after four days of being forced to fight on ground of British choosing, Rommel realised his plan had failed and pulled back. Monty had had his first encounter with the enemy and survived. Immediately morale improved. In his diary, he described his success at holding back Rommel's assault in terms of a tennis match. "I feel I have won the first game – when it was his service. Next time it will be my service, the score being one-love."

His confidence boosted, Monty ignored Churchill's impatient

hectoring and settled down to prepare his forces for the offensive. He built up large reserves of fuel and ammunition; 300 of the latest US Sherman tanks arrived by sea; training exercises were held night and day to familiarise the troops with their new vehicles. He reinforced the artillery batteries on the heights of Alam El Halfa, and forced the air and army headquarters to integrate into a single command, copying the Germans who had used combined air and armour attacks to devastating effect. Meanwhile, Monty travelled from unit to unit, standing in the turret of his armoured car, handing out cigarettes and giving impromptu pep talks.

"Radiate confidence," he would tell his headquarters staff, "that's the first duty of a top commander."

*

In October 1942 my father left the Staff College at Haifa in Palestine to join Monty's headquarters, reporting for duty at the large encampment on the beach at Burg-el-Arab. It had been just over two months since Gott's plane crash. In his diaries, my father offers no explanation as to why Monty had summoned him, but the bond that had grown up between him and his stepfather, particularly since Betty's death, must have exerted some pull. Monty was comforted by Richard's presence, and probably wanted him nearby for the main confrontation with Rommel that he and everyone knew was coming and which would determine Monty's reputation as a general.

"I have my stepson, Dick Carver, joining me this week from the Staff College. I am devoted to him and it will be delightful to have him with me," Monty wrote in a letter home on 12th October 1942.

Monty allowed it to be known that he was planning a southerly hook around the German positions, just as Rommel had tried to do at Alam El Halfa. Only this time it was a feint – instead Monty intended to direct the weight of his attack at the centre of Rommel's lines in the north in the hope of punching two holes through the German defences. Dozens of fake tanks were constructed out of plywood and placed in the desert at the southern end of his frontline, while tanks in the north were covered with canvas to disguise their outline. Ammunition dumps were disguised as piles of trash and a fake pipeline was shown under construction, with the hope that the Germans would be fooled into thinking the Allies were less advanced in their preparations than they were.

In six weeks, Monty built up an army of a quarter of a million troops – easily outnumbering the German forces – and by October 23rd he was ready to go. At nine thirty in the evening, nine hundred guns opened fire along the length of the entire German front – it was the largest artillery bombardment that had ever been mounted by the British army; the battle of El Alamein had begun.

Thanks to the intelligence picked up from Ultra, Monty had been able to time the attack for a moment when Rommel was away in Germany receiving medical treatment. But Monty still faced considerable obstacles – not least the half a million mines the Germans had buried in the sand in what was known as the "Devil's Gardens". The sappers had been sent in as soon as the bombardment ended to clear channels for the tanks to come through. They walked on foot to avoid detonating the heavier anti-tank mines; it was a slow process and soon the British tanks were backed up in traffic jams trying to enter the channels.

Monty threw everything at the German lines in the hope of quickly blowing a hole in the enemy's defences but after three days the positions of each side had hardly changed. A stand-in general from the Russian Front had a heart attack on the field of battle and died. Hitler ordered Rommel out of his sanatorium and back into the frontline. As soon as he returned, Rommel immediately understood that the main attack was in the north and ordered reinforcements into the area. For a moment, it looked as if the British might fail.

Haunted by the failures of Monty's predecessors, Churchill

fell into despair. "Is it really impossible to find a general who can win a battle?" he is said to have yelled at his staff in disgust on October 26th.

When it seemed that the frontal assault was not going to cut the German army in half as he'd hoped, Monty began to consider changing tactics. He was loathe to switch his approach in the middle of the battle but he could see that Rommel, with his back to the sea in the north, was going to fight ferociously and he knew that failure was not an option.

On October 29th, he launched Operation Supercharge. The idea was to keep the Germans engaged in the north but to redeploy Allied reserves to the south and use them to come in behind the main part of the Deutsch Afrika Korps rather than to attempt to cut them in half. The RAF had succeeded in sinking three German tankers in the Mediterranean and the German tanks were running short of petrol, reducing their room for manoeuvre.

For his part, stuck at headquarters, Richard saw little of the actual fighting, but he could follow what was happening by listening to the radio traffic. After five days, the mood began to lighten slightly. The Allies had new tanks and plenty of fuel and ammunition while the Germans were tired and their equipment, having travelled so far, was beginning to fray.

Monty gave the task of encircling the German forces to the 10th Corps, commanded by General Herbert Lumsden. 10th Corps was Monty's mobile reserve – his *Corps de Chasse* as he called it – and had been designed to move fast. As other Corps kept the German forces back and protected his flanks, General Lumsden was told to take his tanks as quickly as possible across the desert and attack the enemy positions from the rear.

Monty had concerns about Lumsden. The night before he launched Supercharge, he had confessed in his diary, "Lumsden has been very disappointing; he may be better when we get out into the open. But my own view is that he is not suited for high command, but is a good fighting Div commander. He is excitable,

**Monty watching his troops advance towards German lines,
North Africa, 1942**

**Monty with his three corps commanders –from left: Lt-Generals
Leese and Lumsden and Horrocks**

highly strung and is easily depressed. He is considerably at sea in charge of a Corps and I have to watch over him very carefully."

He would have preferred someone else to lead the charge but it was too late to change commanders now. He posted one of his own liaison officers to Lumsden's staff to keep an eye on him and to ensure that he remained in constant contact. Once they had set off, the officer discovered that each time he stopped to set up his desert aerial, Lumsden would order his troops to move before he had been able to make contact with Monty's HQ. Monty had little idea where his commander was.

Operation Supercharge did not go to plan. But it nonetheless succeeded in finally breaking the will of the German forces. Lumsden's tanks, helped by the air force, picked off the German tanks that had been forced out into the open to fight, some of which were immobilised having run out of fuel.

By the evening of 2nd November, the situation was looking dire for Rommel. His armoured commanders reported that they had less than 100 tanks left, compared to 600 or so British tanks. He realised that the famous Deutsche Afrika Korps was in danger of being annihilated.

At 8pm that evening, the Ultra code-breakers at Bletchley Park outside London intercepted a situation report from Rommel to the German High Command in Berlin. It contained an unmistakable air of defeat and gloom – and was the first suggestion that Rommel was considering a retreat: "After ten days of extremely hard fighting against overwhelming British superiority on the ground and in the air the strength of the Army is exhausted in spite of today's successful defence... there is only one road available, and the army, as it passes along it, will almost certainly be attacked day and night by the enemy air force."

That night after reading the message, Churchill celebrated with a cigar, while out in the cold undulating desert, Rommel lay on his bunk-bed with his forces scattered for hundreds of miles around him. "I lie with my eyes open and rack my brain for a way out of this disaster for our troops. Difficult days lie ahead of us; perhaps the most difficult for any man to live through," he wrote in his diary. At the German High Command in Berlin, Rommel's message was greeted by silence. Hearing nothing back, Rommel told Berendt his liaison officer the next day to formally ask Hitler for permission to withdraw.

Hitler sent his response back to his commander: "In your present situation, nothing else can be thought of but to hold on, not to yield a step. Throw every man and every gun into battle… as to your troops, you can show them no other road than that to victory or death."

This was madness. Rommel pleaded with Hitler to be allowed to pull back: "We cannot stand and fight. Thousands of the troops do not even have rifles."

"That is because they have thrown them away," Hitler taunted a few minutes later. The telegrams travelled back and forward, silently monitored by the eavesdroppers of Bletchley. That night, ignoring his Führer's order to fight to the death, Rommel told his commanders to start pulling back along the road which they had used to advance so swiftly a few months before.

"I envy the dead," Rommel wrote in his diary, "for them it is all over."

On 4th November General von Thoma, commander of the German armoured corps, jumped on top of one of his tanks and drove into the centre of the battle to assess the situation. Von Thoma had survived the bloody battle of Verdun in the First World War and had led the first Nazi troops into Poland. He was a man known for his icy demeanour, yet he was realistic.

For two days it had been clear to him that they were beaten: his troops were under constant attack from the air and were being attacked by wave after wave of fresh British forces that Monty had held in reserve; there was hardly any petrol and he had lost 500 out of his 600 tanks.

At the top of the little hill of Tel el Mampsra his tank took a

**The surrender of General Wilhelm von Thoma,
on 4th November 1942**

direct hit. The German general got out and stood calmly beside the wreckage. All around him lay the bodies of his soldiers and a sea of burning vehicles. *Sieg oder Tod*. Twenty minutes later, a passing British captain in the 10th Hussars arrested him and took him back to Monty's headquarters.

As Monty emerged from his caravan, von Thoma saluted and offered his surrender. Making sure there was an official photographer on hand to capture the moment, Monty then invited the German general to dinner. Once the meal was cleared away, Monty lay out on the white tablecloth the situation as he saw it using the salt and pepper as his forces. Von Thoma was surprised by how much Monty knew about the positions of the German forces. Even more so to learn from Monty that British forces had reached the town of Fuka.

"*Sehr kritisch, wirklich sehr kritisch*, (That's critical, very critical)" the German general kept saying. But it wasn't true. Monty was bluffing.

That evening, Monty gave his generals new orders. Rommel might be retreating but he was still free and much of his forces were intact. Monty knew that this would be no more than a temporary victory if he allowed Rommel to escape and fight on.

His plan was to get 30th Corps to race through the night across the desert to get to Fuka before Rommel and block his exit – thereby making his comment to von Thoma come true. This would trap Rommel's army on a 40-mile stretch of the coast road.

"We will block the bottle," Monty declared. Once that had happened, General Lumsden and his Corps de Chasse would be offered the chance to redeem themselves by sweeping in from the desert to crush the German forces against the anvil of the sea.

As his stepfather sketched out his battle plan on the sand, Richard stood in the background among the sand dunes facing the sea with the other liaison officers and the intelligence majors, listening to him. He was excited at the prospect of advancing. Suddenly there was a rattle of a machine gun nearby. Thinking it was a Messerschmitt, the generals and the junior officers dived under their vehicles, but it turned out to be the British tank gunner on sentry duty down the beach. He had opened fire at a flock of Teal ducks heading down the coast. Several of the birds fell nearby and Monty's cook collected them and served them to the generals for dinner.

By now it was clear to the world that the British had scored a major victory. For the first time since the start of the Second World War, it was the Germans who were on the run not the Allies and there was no question that Hitler's desert army had been defeated.

It had been three years since the Second World War had begun and in Britain, people had grown used to an unending diet of bad news – the fall of Poland, the collapse of Belgium and Holland, the retreat from Dunkirk, the occupation of Paris, the fall of Singapore – but on November 5th they woke to unaccustomed headlines on the radio and in the newspapers.

"Axis Forces in full Retreat: Official," proclaimed the *Daily Telegraph*. Churchill ordered church bells to be rung across the country.

"Before El Alamein, we never had a victory, after El Alamein we never had a defeat," he later boasted. In America, news of the victory briefly pushed the presidential election off the front page.

That morning, the 5th, after giving von Thoma breakfast and waving him off into captivity, Monty called a press conference on the beach.

"The enemy is completely smashed," he declared. "But we must not think that the party is over. We have no intention of letting the enemy recover. We must keep up the pressure. We intend to hit this chap for six out of North Africa."

At first it looked like the Breakout plan might work; the first radio reports suggested the advancing forces could see the lights of the town of Fuka. But the reports turned out to be wrong. In the chaos of the previous night an entire division had stopped for several hours instead of racing forwards and elsewhere hundreds of tanks, confused by the maze of minefields and dummy minefields and drained by two weeks of fighting, turned east inside of west.

Lumsden failed to keep in regular contact once more and again, Monty had little idea where he was. By the time his 10th Corps had reached the coastal road, Rommel had already passed. A few hours later, the Ultra intercepts arrived, showing that Rommel had reached Fuka without any serious difficulties. He had slipped through the net.

"It was a wild helter-skelter drive through another pitch black night," Rommel wrote in his diary.

Over the weeks, the headquarters at Burg-el-Arab had turned into a sprawling Bedouin-like encampment amidst the sand dunes between the coastal road and the sea. The site consisted of about forty vehicles which were spread out over the sand dunes to minimise the casualties in the event of an air attack. Each clump of vehicles was drawn up in a square providing a protected area in the middle to work. The maps of the battle were hung on the outsides of the vehicles and a camouflage net was thrown over the top to give protection from the sun and to disguise the vehicles from enemy aircraft. Monty's two caravans stood off slightly to one side. Footpaths had been worn in the sand from the Tac HQ to the Main HQ to the mess tents and down to the latrines which sat on the beach facing out to sea.

Richard was an Ops Officer in the headquarters. After only three weeks in the desert he was still a greenhorn, very conscious that there were men all around him who had retreated with the Eighth Army all the way from Tunis, enduring defeat after defeat at the hands of Rommel. He could see that for them this battle was personal and that they were determined to get revenge.

Throughout the battle of El Alamein he helped to keep the headquarters operating: organising briefings, updating the maps, fetching commanders, getting intelligence delivered to the forward positions, and helping with the logistics of the "village". The days of the battle passed in a blur of stress, orders, counter-orders and frayed tempers, all accompanied by the terror of "messing up".

At the height of the battle, the headquarters found themselves in the middle of the artillery lines. Some of the guns were in front, others were behind firing over their heads, for two days and nights the noise of the barrage from the "25 pounders" had made sleep impossible. Eventually the tide of battle turned in their favour, the guns were moved forward and the sound of the radios and the generators returned once more.

As a captain in the frontline Richard would have had 100 men to look after at most. Yet here he was surrounded by generals responsible for tens of thousands of lives and millions of tons of equipment – Leese, Freyberg, Gatehouse, Lumsden – all coming back and forth to receive their orders.

They would drive their scout cars into the encampment and

jump out, accompanied by their ADC and Intelligence Officer, their faces drained by lack of sleep, their tank goggles and uniforms coated in thick dust and vehicle grease. Richard saw his stepfather almost every day at meetings and briefings, but Monty was careful not to treat Richard any differently from any of the other young officers.

As the advance progressed, the tension began to ease slightly at the headquarters. The danger of being overrun or bombed by the Germans diminished and in their spare moments, Richard and the others sat on the beach smoking and reliving what they had just gone through. They felt sure that this was a moment that would be talked about for generations and taught in British history.

Richard was there the day that Monty, frustrated by Lumsden's unreliable behaviour, pulled him out of the front line and ordered him back to base. When Lumsden arrived, he was told to report immediately to Monty's caravan. A shouting match ensued, with Lumsden arguing that it was the Army Commander's job to visit his commanders in the field not the other way round. The exchange could be heard outside by Richard and the others. Some of the headquarters officers who had worked in the City before the war, had created an informal "stock exchange" chart showing the fortunes of each of the field commanders like shares.

"Sell Lumsdens," someone said.

His stock was marked down to the bottom of the chart. Lumsden walked out of Monty's caravan and noticed the board in the command post. Lifting the cover from it which read "Most Secret", Lumsden saw that his stock had plummeted.

4.

IF MONTY COULD not sack Lumsden, he could at least keep a much closer eye on him. So he decided to move his headquarters up as close to the frontline as possible. On November 5th, he ordered Richard to take a staff car and drive 60 miles forward to Daba, to reconnoitre a new position for the headquarters. Richard traveled blithely up the coast road in an open car without any armoured protection, accompanied by his driver with a sten gun. Only 48 hours before, thousands of German troops had been dug in all along the road. Richard stared in awe at the detritus of a defeated army that was strewn across the desert – discarded helmets, guns, tents, tanks and artillery guns still smouldering with the occasional charred bodies of the crew. It was his first sight of how ferocious the battle had been.

Most of the Allied forces were ten miles south in the desert attempting to outflank the Germans. The road was clogged with fuel trucks, mess wagons, tank recovery vehicles, ambulances and ammunition wagons all rumbling slowly forward, trying to keep pace with the advance. Richard waved at each convoy as they overtook

– it felt good to be part of a victorious army.

At Daba, he chose a site that looked much like Burg-el-Arab, between the road and the coast. As he walked across the dunes looking for a flat piece of ground he was startled to discover that the enemy was still there. He wrote in his green leather notebook:

There were still Italians in trenches and dugouts among the sand dunes who came out and gave themselves up quite readily. I sent about 200 back to the road under our own military police. They were a miserable looking lot and I felt contemptuous rather than sorry for them.

As he drove back through the moonless night, passing the convoys going the other way, their lights dimmed, Richard could not have imagined that 36 hours later he himself would be a prisoner. At the headquarters, he gathered together the small collection of vehicles that made up Monty's Tac or Forward HQ, including the General's two caravans, and led them patiently back down the road to Daba. It was dawn on the morning of the 6th before he had guided them into place.

Monty awoke on the morning of the 6th to discover that once again his forces had failed to trap the Desert Fox. He was told that several of his divisions had halted to rest overnight. A mixture of exhaustion and lethargy was creeping in – by now every soldier in the Eighth Army knew that they had won and that Rommel was in retreat. The incentive to fight was less critical. Monty's order to 'move by night and fight by day' was clearly not being followed.

On top of that, the constant changing of objectives was causing confusion among the units, hampered furthered by the growing distances which made radio communication difficult. They had advanced more than sixty miles since El Alamein. The Sherman tanks donated by the Americans consumed a gallon of fuel every three miles and were beginning to run out of petrol. Monty began to fear that his orderly annihilation of Rommel's forces was turning into a disorderly rout. He was trying to "plug the bath" as he called it, but each time he ordered his forces to lunge forward, Rommel managed to move quicker.

Lumsden's new orders had been to secure the ancient Ptolemaic port of Mersa Metruh that was on both the road and the railway line that ran along the coast. If the British could get there before Rommel, they could separate the German army from its supply lines. But according to intelligence sources, Rommel had reached the port and was already hungrily emptying the quay of supplies as well as the couple of ships that had evaded the Allied blockade in the Mediterranean.

Monty arrived at Daba and approved the new position for his headquarters that Richard had found, before driving further up the coast road to get to the "tip of the spear". When he reached the forward positions of his army, Monty could see groups of Allied tanks halted in the desert. He asked why they were not advancing and was told that some were waiting for the fuel trucks to come through, others had been delayed by a German anti-tank battery.

Around midday, the sky suddenly darkened and lightning started to flare over the sea. A cool wind began to whip up the sand and a few moments later the air was filled with the unfamiliar sound of raindrops pounding on the hard desert. The radio officer told Monty that the electricity in the air was playing havoc with the delicate crystal radio sets and that communication was becoming increasingly difficult.

Monty ordered all units to pass on a message to Lumsden to get in touch: COMMANDER 10 CORPS MUST MEET THE ARMY COMMANDER AT 835321 LATE AFTERNOON. Monty drove out in his staff car to the spot in the desert but Lumsden never showed up.

At the headquarters at Daba, Richard felt the first raindrops about the same time as Monty did. He hurried with everyone else to put the maps and radio equipment back into the armoured command vehicles. The meteorologists said that it would be a passing shower, but the rain kept coming down all afternoon. By about five o'clock, the RAF declared that they'd been forced to call off their bombing raids as their desert airstrip had become unusable. All around the battlefield, the desert had started to turn into grey mud.

Sheltering inside the mess tent, Richard wrote in his notebook:

> *Nov 6th. Monty came back in the evening having been up in his tank to within 20 miles of Mersa Matruh…. Alex* [General Harold Alexander, the Commander-in-Chief of Middle East forces], *arrived about 9pm and I took him down to Monty's caravan on the sea-shore; but Monty had already retired to bed and Alex refused to disturb him; but went off to his own caravan which I had put some distance away.*

Monty wanted to keep on the move. Intelligences reports came through suggesting that Rommel was pulling out of Mersa Matruh. They seemed to confirm Monty's suspicions that Rommel would use the cover of darkness to retreat west towards the Libyan border. Before turning in, he left orders for Richard to find a new location for the HQ another 60 miles further forward, beyond Mersa Matruh. As Richard noted:

> *He thought the Germans wouldn't stop short of the Sollum escarpment and he ordered us to go up the following day and establish Army HQ the other side of Matruh.*

Exhausted and hungry, Richard sat in the mess tent that evening of the 6th November listening to the rain. The command vehicles were up to their ankles in mud. He couldn't see how they could be moved.

Hugh Mainwaring [the head of the Headquarters staff]

told me I would have to take the Advance Party again, leaving at 0200am and he would come with me. My car had had a puncture and although my driver was pretty tired I made him repair it that night in the LO's tent. We set off at 0200 after a little difficulty in contacting the remainder of the Advance Party.

It was raining heavily and in the dark we evidently passed through the two Armoured Divisions bogged down in the mud on either side of the road. Anyhow we saw very little on the road, except for the smouldering vehicles left by the Germans which we thought our Air had destroyed.

If it had been risky for Richard to have gone up to Daba the day before, it was considerably more hazardous for him to be traveling another sixty miles west – the place where Monty wanted Richard to position his new headquarters was further forward than his own Divisional Commanders. Monty was determined to show his commanders how to lead from the front; but he had only a sketchy idea how far down the road Rommel's forces were and Richard had even less.

The intelligence reports turned out to be wrong; Rommel had decided to stay in Mersa Matruh overnight. Two officers, one of whom was the stepson of the man who had just shattered the Third Reich's aura of invincibility, were driving towards three hundred thousand German soldiers armed only with pistols.

*

About 7am we were held up by a flooded nala [a dry river bed] *but I managed to get my car across with the help of an RAF tender… We inspected a possible site near the Bagush turning and then went on about half a mile until we came to another flooded nala. I was driving and as we dipped down into this nala I saw a truck drawn up on the left of the road with Germans in it. At first I thought they were our prisoners; but they shouted at us to stop and turned their guns on us and then I realised that we were caught.*

It was a terrible moment, possibly the worst in my life – that awful sinking feeling as one realised that one had been captured and there was nothing one could do about it. I couldn't drive on as the nala had water in it and there was another German truck approaching from the other side and of course I couldn't turn around. In a couple of seconds some Germans had jumped out of their truck and were waving pistols in our faces and shouting at us to get out. There was nothing for it but to comply.

I made an effort to get my coat out of the back of the car but they wouldn't let me, saying something about the car following. We were pushed into the back of an open eight-seater and at once drove off with a big ugly-looking lieutenant standing facing us, leaning against the windscreen with a pistol in his hand. We drove back at great speed; I had no greatcoat and felt pretty cold though mercifully I was wearing my battledress. All the time I was weighing up in my mind what were the chances of making a successful getaway then as against the possibility of being re-captured or the chances of escaping later on.

Innumerable times I measured the distance between myself and the lieutenant, wondering whether I could catch him a clip on the chin before he fired his revolver into my stomach. There were German soldiers in the truck besides the driver, but I thought we could probably deal with them if we knocked the lieutenant out. But a really favourable opportunity never presented itself, so we arrived at Deutsche Afrika Korps HQ which at that time was south of Mersa. We could see tanks of the DAK engaged in an armoured battle about 2000 yards to the south, but unfortunately our fellows did not penetrate any nearer that day.

It was about 10.30am when we arrived at the HQ and I had had only a biscuit since 0200 so when they offered some sandwiches and ersatz coffee I found it very welcome and so did my driver. Hugh would only take a little coffee. After about an hour they took us over to the Intelligence Staff Officer's caravan where we were searched and interrogated. They had taken my notebook from me whilst I was trying to get rid of it on the truck and I regret to say it contained some names of officers in the Eighth Army. This made me feel more miserable than ever.

Sitting on the bench outside the Intelligence Officer's caravan, Richard wondered anxiously how much information Rommel's Intelligence Corps had about Monty. Would they know that he had a son and two stepsons? Did they know what their names were or where they were serving? Monty had only very recently risen to the top levels of the British army. Richard hoped that the intelligence dossier on him had not yet been fully assembled.

I thought we were in for a stiff interrogation but after the usual formal questions (name, rank and number and unit, which we didn't give) the IO shut up and amazing to say we were never questioned again. The Germans always wear their decorations in the full and this Intelligence Staff Officer was an amazing sight in the middle of the desert having some large green star on his breast and something else around his neck. We were then asked if we needed baths and said 'No', so we continued to sit outside the IO's caravan in the sun and at last I began to feel warm. About 1400 we were put on a truck and taken off to Panzer Armee HQ which was then not far from Sollum.

The fact that he had a different name from Monty had saved Richard. The Germans never made the connection. Had they done so, the High Command would almost certainly have ordered Richard to be flown to Berlin and kept as hostage as a way of demoralising Monty. Inside the thick walls of Colditz Castle the Germans had already collected an odd assortment of Allied relatives and offspring including a nephew of Churchill and the son of Field Marshal Haig.

Twelve hundred miles away, at the Lord Mayor's luncheon at the Mansion House in the City of London, Churchill celebrated the victory of El Alamein. "This is not the end, it is not even the beginning of the end. But it is perhaps the end of the beginning," he intoned. Churchill was right; El Alamein and the far bloodier defeat of Hitler's army which was occurring at Stalingrad at the same time proved to be the tipping point. Though the Second World War still had another 30 months to run, the German army never regained the upper hand from that moment on.

*

That night – November 7th 1942 – Rommel pulled his forces out of Mersa Matruh. Richard and Hugh spent the night lying in a six foot by six foot trench guarded by two sentries.

> *I didn't care much about sleep but thought only of the possibilities of escape. They seemed to be pretty poor, as it was a bright night and we had two sentries over us. In the morning when we thought we would drift slowly back through POW cages, we were taken instead to an aerodrome and flown back to Tobruk. There was the usual dust storm blowing and I thought we might be able to creep off in it but we were very closely guarded. We were taken to the Control Hut where we waited for about an hour.*
>
> *Then we were taken out again under guard of a really unpleasant Nazi NCO who looked hate in every pore. Indian prisoners were being made to carry petrol about and they looked pretty miserable. We were pushed into a transport plane which was carrying empty petrol tins. It wasn't very comfortable and when we got high up it was pretty cold. Our guard and rear gunner gave us some ersatz chocolate which was very good and some biscuits. After five hours flying we came down over flat country covered in olive groves which I thought looked like the heel of Italy and I was right.*

Richard and Hugh were taken to a large holding camp outside Brindisi where there was an argument between the Germans and the Italians over what to do with them since the camp was for soldiers and not officers. Eventually the Italians decided to keep them separate and put them in the sick bay in recognition of their officer status. An Italian guard came in and asked them what they would like for dinner:

We nearly fell down in astonishment but recovered sufficiently to agree to a large plate of macaroni stew, bread, cheese and vino.

It was the best meal they had had in several days, but after they had eaten, gloom descended. It was a violent shock to be removed so suddenly from the noise of battle and the frenetic activity of the headquarters, just when victory was in their grasp. Richard lay in the sick bay, going over and over the moment of his capture in his mind and thinking how he could have avoided it. He imagined Monty and the headquarters pushing forward, leaving the two of them further and further behind.

We were now well and truly captives, locked up in a small room in a camp surrounded by barbed wire and guarded by sentries in the enemy's country. Up until that time we had been kept on the move and as long as were on the move there had always seemed to be some hope of escape however remote, but now it would mean a long and arduous job probably to get out of camp and then the almost insuperable task of getting out of the country. We were doomed to the life of a POW for some time, possibly even for years!

The next morning they were ordered downstairs where they found a horse-drawn cart with a driver waiting in the rain. They squashed into the back with their guards and the cart ambled off; as they passed out of the hospital gates the reins of knotted rope broke, forcing everyone to dismount while they were repaired. By the time they arrived at Brindisi railway station, guards and prisoners alike were soaked through. From Brindisi they travelled in a first class compartment ninety miles up the Adriatic coast to the small port of Bari.

It was dark by the time they got there and no one had any idea where they were supposed to go, so they waited on the platform with their guards. Eventually a small boy on a bicycle appeared out of the darkness.

We set off walking through the dark wet streets guided by the little boy and carrying our bundles, a lugubrious little procession. In the dark the boy lost the way and took us such a long way round that by the time we did eventually arrive at the camp we had walked about 10 km and the guards cursed the boy heartily.

The new camp was a miserable-looking compound of huts surrounded by two rows of barbed wire. Richard and Hugh were shoved into a long single storey hut with no glass in the windows. The next morning they woke to see clumps of grey figures with blankets draped over their shoulders pacing around inside the wire. They learnt that they were in a transit camp, where they were supposed to be for only a few weeks. But some of the inmates, it turned out, had been there several months, awaiting deportation to other camps.

The conditions were grim; the single electric bulb was too dim to read by and the cold weather made them permanently hungry. Many of the inmates were still dressed in the thin shirts and shorts they had been captured in in the desert. For breakfast they were given a small helping of stewed onions and ersatz coffee; for lunch they had a bread roll and a thin soup made out of pumpkin and the same for supper.

If Monty had any regrets about ordering his stepson on such a foolhardy mission, he didn't share them with anyone. After all, he had been only 24 hours out in his assessment: Rommel had pulled out of Mersa Matruh on the night of 7th rather than the 6th. But his private correspondence revealed his sadness at losing Richard; on 8th November 1942 he wrote to David's guardian,

Phyllis Reynolds, in England: "I regret to say that my stepson Dick Carver was captured by the Germans at Matruh on 7th November. He was on a forward reconnaissance in the early morning. I am very sad about it as I was devoted to him and he to me. Would you make enquiries through the Red Cross as to where he is? When we know where he is we must arrange for a proper and regular despatch of parcels; but it is too early to do that yet; we must first locate his prison camp."

*

I suppose someone must have lent us a razor as I remember shaving...

The next few days in Richard's diary are written as if they were in a dream as he struggled to comprehend that he was really a prisoner of war. No one had any idea how long the war would drag on or what would happen to them. Even if they managed to escape, where would they go – they were stuck in enemy territory separated by the sea from their colleagues in the Eighth Army and hundreds of miles from England. The best they could hope for is that Monty would sweep through North Africa and then turn his attention to Italy, but it seemed a long shot.

Richard found the best way to cope with the depression was not to think about freedom or the past but to focus on the present and how to improve the conditions in their hut. They fashioned a mess table by taking one board from each person's bunk then add-ing a table cloth – a rough piece of hessian – and some knives and forks. One corner of the room they allocated as the 'card room' for gambling. At the other end, they held lectures; each prisoner was given the opportunity to describe their capture and their version of the battle as they saw it. The chance to explain offered a form of therapy. In syndicates of fives they shared a razor, a mirror and a comb. They appointed a Captain Mickelthwait to pester the camp commandant for changes to their standard of living.

One day the commandant surprised them by agreeing to hear their complaints. All 150 officers turned up and Captain

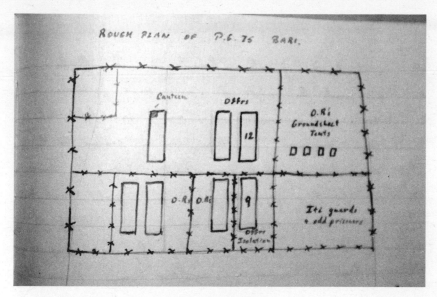

PG75, at Bari

Mickelthwait, speaking through an interpreter, listed their grievances as 1. Clothes. 2. Red cross parcels. 3. If this was a transit camp, shouldn't they be moved on? 4. The poor conditions in the tented accommodation where the Other Ranks were housed.

Since the interpreter was clearly telling the commandant something very different to what he was hearing, it was a fruitless conversation until the commandant agreed to let one of the officers speak directly to him in Italian.

> *An officer stood up who could speak Italian and let him have it.*
> *The commandant began gesticulating and getting furious. Finally*
> *the officer said that we treated the Italian prisoners much better in*
> *England than they were treating us, whereupon the Comandante*
> *pretty well lost his head and certainly his temper and the meeting*
> *broke up in chaos. The next day we heard that 30 officers were to be*
> *moved to another camp forthwith. Whether this order was a sequel*
> *to our meeting we never knew.*

On 29th of November – three weeks after his capture – Richard was among the 30 who were marched back to the railway station and put on a train. His spirits immediately lifted: "we were all like schoolboys for we felt the change couldn't be for the worse."

The train took them from Bari over the snow covered Apennines. It was exhilarating to sit and watch the scenery go by; just to be on the move once more gave Richard hope. As they trundled along, the senior Italian officer in charge of the guards gave them an impromptu lecture on the theme of *"povera Italia"* and how she had been forced into the war because she had no raw materials of her own and the Allies were blockading her. From Naples they travelled slowly north up the coast, passing through Rome in the middle of the night, until finally reaching the town of Arezzo forty miles south of Florence just as dawn was breaking.

At Arezzo, they were ordered out and caught a little train that chugged up the Arno valley to Poppi, their final destination. As they were marched from the station, they could see the twelfth-century castle built by the Guidi family which towered over the red roofs of the town. They stopped outside a large building on top of a nearby hill surrounded by tall cypresses. The name above the doorway announced that it had once been a convent called the Villa Ascensione. It seemed an incongruous name for a prisoner of war camp. They were greeted by four British officers, Lt Commander Bowker, Captain Turner, Flight Lieutenant Spence and Flt Lt Pringlewood, who turned out to be virtually the only inmates of the camp. A few weeks earlier a large New Zealand detachment had been moved out.

To our astonishment, the Italian authorities served us cocoa and biscuits as soon as we got in the door. We soon discovered that this was a very different place to Bari. In fact in contrast to that stinking place it appeared a perfect paradise. There were Red Cross parcels and a limited amount of clothing. We had beds with mattresses and slept in dormitories of 6. There was a little garden inside the wire with the basketball pitch and a short exercise path.

Richard liked the intimacy of the camp – there were only 90 prisoners, a big contrast to the large impersonal transit camp. The trauma of the capture was receding and he was drawn by the beauty of where he had ended up. He had never been to Italy before and he began to take a close interest in his surroundings. He asked one of the Italian guards to teach him about the area. From the top floor windows, the guard pointed out the medieval walled town of Poppi in the north dominated by the old castello where Dante was thought to have lived and to have written the *Divine Comedy*. In the east they looked across water meadows and an undulating landscape of farms and vineyards down into the valley to La Verna where the guard said St Francis had received his stigmata; in the south lay Bibbiena in front of a range of snow capped mountains. It was a strange place to be a prisoner. He knew that he was fortunate compared to many others.

To his surprise, Richard found that he almost enjoyed the routine of camp life. The food was sufficient. He could rest and

The town of Poppi, with Villa Ascensione, the prison camp, in front

read. While others were itching to escape and continue the war, he welcomed the peace and isolation. The odd traditions of the place – all the meals were announced by Flight Lieutenant Pringlewood bellowing 'Tallyho!" at the top of his voice – the communal dining, the similarities of class and backgrounds and the routines of study reminded him of being back at Cambridge as an undergraduate.

"We developed something of a family spirit," he wrote approvingly in his diary. Somehow he managed to keep a list of all the officers in Prigionie di Guerra (PG) 38, carrying it through all the adventures that he subsequently endured, at some risk to himself and those on the list. He recorded their regiments and even their nicknames: "Pop" Morrison. "Fanny" Fane-Hervey and a Colonel MacDonnell who was known as "The Gloomy Dean".

Richard was asked to be "Professor of Studies" and "Officiating Padre" which he was happy to do. He organised two lectures a week in farming, French, German, Arabic, and Italian.

We held our first service on Christmas Day in the dining room. I chalked the words of the hymns up on the ping-pong table, for we had only one hymn-book in the camp and only one Army prayer-book. Jimmy Hannah played the piano and Hugh read the lessons. I gave a short address. There was a very good attendance, I think about half the camp so I was encouraged to go on. After that I took the service every Sunday until Palm Sunday when padres Lawrence and Guinness took over.

At Christmas I insisted on putting up decorations and with the help of others in my room we made a very good show of the dining room. Coloured paper from the Red Cross parcels was used for streamers and branches of fir trees hung on the walls. I painted a little menu card for each table.

Richard's insistence on decorating the Villa showed how at home he felt there. He had ceased to see it as a prison. But he was aware that others did not share the same enthusiasm and he was careful to continue joining in the heated discussions that took place about how and when to escape. There had been several attempts in the past. Some had tried to climb out of the windows on the side of the Villa that faced the road where the barbed wire ran very close to the house. Two had escaped that way by climbing down knotted sheets only to be recaptured after three days. A mad parachutist had had the idea of running out of one of the windows off a plank and over the sentry's head using a sheet as an impromptu parachute to break his fall but he'd somehow never found the right moment.

It was decided that the only feasible way out was to sink a shaft down into the floor of the dining room and dig a passageway through a door in the outside wall which was half concealed below ground and out into the garden. That would get them past the first line of wire. They would then be able to get over the second wire under darkness. It was slow and tiring work since all they had to dig with was an old table knife and a broken spade. They kept a table covered in a tablecloth nearby that they could quickly move over the hole if the lookout warned that guards were on the way. They seldom managed more than a couple of hours a day.

Disposal of the soil was the main difficulty. First we tried the garden but the 'Caribs' [the Carabinieri, the Italian police who helped to guard the camps] *began to take too much of an interest. After that we had to carry it all the way up to the top floor in Red Cross boxes and deposit it under the floor boards of the attic.*

One afternoon, they noticed the Comandante scrutinizing the half submerged doorway on the outside wall. He appeared to be looking for some evidence of tampering; perhaps the guards had been tipped off. The Comandante went inside and down into the dining room. They just had time to pull Richard out of the tunnel and move the table and tablecloth over the hole in the floor. Richard sat at the table, with earth under his fingernails, conscious of the Comandante examining him closely. Eventually without saying anything the Comandante turned and left. Richard was sure he suspected something and that it was only the fear of being laughed at if he was wrong that had stopped him peering underneath the tablecloth.

*

By February 1943 – three months after Richard's disappearance – Monty still had no idea what had happened to his stepson beyond the fact that he'd been captured. The lack of news was causing considerable concern in the family. As they tried to find out from the Red Cross what had happened, it opened up an old dispute about who was Richard's next of kin. Was it his elder brother John who was his closest blood relative, or Monty who was his only legal parent?

On February 20th 1943 on the eve of the battle of Medenine, Monty wrote indignantly to the Reynoldses, David's guardians: "It is complete nonsense the way everyone goes on about next-of-kin to Dick Carver. As his step-father I am legally his next of kin. In any case it is far better that I should handle it, as my name will probably get things done much quicker than anyone else. So you carry on doing it all, and tell everyone else it is my order that you should do it."

By now Monty had pushed Rommel back through Egypt and Libya and was close to cornering him at Tunis. After failing to break out of the Eighth Army encirclement at Medenine, Rommel resigned his post at the head of the fabled Deutsche Afrika Korps on 10th March 1943 and left Africa never to return. The DAK surrendered two months later.

By the end of April the tunnel was down about 10 feet and had reached the foundations but to their disappointment they found the doorway had been bricked up on the inside. Just then it was announced that PG38 was to be broken up. The prisoners decided to leave the tunnel intact just in case there were further arrivals.

As they were emptying the last of the Red Cross boxes of earth in the attic, one of the men, trying to compress the spoil, stamped too hard.

That afternoon the ceiling began to show enormous cracks and suddenly whilst I was watching a section of about 50 feet gave way and came down with a colossal bang! Everyone thought it was a terrific joke except the Italians who hoped they had got through our six months term without any "unpleasant" incidents.

They told the Comandante that the earth came from an old tunnel dug by the previous group of New Zealand prisoners before the Comandante had arrived. When he asked why the soil looked so new, they told him that the attic was airtight and had kept it remarkably fresh. He demanded proof that this had not come from a new excavation so all the earth was carried back downstairs and packed into the New Zealanders' tunnel in the commandant's presence. It just about fitted and honour was satisfied.

On 28th May, two days after Richard's 29th birthday, the entire camp was marched to the railway station back down the hill they had come up six months earlier. Richard was glad to be on the move once more but he knew that he was unlikely ever to have such a pleasant internment as he had had at Poppi in the Tuscan countryside. As they chugged slowly north in the prison train through the hot Italian countryside, the prisoners discussed the war and what it all meant. An invasion of Italy could not be far off. From Tunis, the Allies could reach Sicily easily. Soon they would be free.

Outside Florence they sat for several hours in a siding as the sun roasted the metal roofs of the carriages. The windows had been sealed shut to prevent escapes and the blinds pulled down. A guard walked through the crowded compartments with a large metal container of water. Each prisoner was allocated one ladleful. In the late afternoon they moved off once more. Finally long after dark the train slowed to a stop, the doors were flung open and they were ordered out onto the empty platforms of a large station. The signs said Bologna. They had been in the carriages for sixteen hours.

The prisoners were divided up. The officers were ordered into the station's main waiting-room where they lay on the floor under close guard. The lower ranks were taken away to another train. At first light the group was split again: the more junior officers were put on one train, which someone said was destined for Modena. The rest, including Richard, were pushed back onboard the train that they had arrived in.

This time the journey was much shorter. It was still well before midday when they pulled into a little station called Castelguelfo, outside the town of Fontanellato. Waiting for them on the platform was a tall Italian officer in his late forties surrounded by carabinieri and a detachment of guards from the Alpini Regiment, Italy's well respected mountain troops. "I am Colonello Eugenio Vicedomini, the commandant of PG49," the officer said in heavily accented English. "And this is Capitano Communio, my chief interpreter."

He nodded at a diminutive figure standing next to him. The two groups – the Italian prison guards and the English officers – eyed each other warily. Richard could see, from the way that Vice-domini held himself and the smart turnout of his troops that he was a professional career soldier and not a conscript.

We marched the four miles to the camp along the hot and dusty road. The countryside appeared quite pleasant though very flat; but we were disappointed when we got to the camp. We had been led to expect a small select senior officers' camp and judging by the name of the station, we thought it might be in the ancient Castello of the Guelphs. What we found was an enormous red-brick orphanage building surrounded by much wire and with hundreds of faces looking out of the windows.

5.

THE FIRST TIME I heard the name Fontanellato was in August 1972, when I was 11. The previous winter, my mother had had a near fatal bout of appendicitis. Her appendix was so swollen that when the doctor removed it in an emergency operation, he asked if he could keep it as a specimen to show his students. When she finally emerged from hospital, she lay at home for several months before suggesting that we should splash out on a family holiday to Italy and Greece to help her recuperate.

We crossed the Channel in the rain, the stench of diesel and the roll of the car ferry making me vomit. It was the first time I had ever left England. Our car was a green Morris Marina which possessed a malevolent spirit. To get it started in the winter my father would have to put its spark plugs in the kitchen stove to dry out, then give the alternator a gentle massage to coax it into cooperating with the spark plugs. All the way across the Channel, my father fretted about whether it would start when we reached the other side. He was terrified of "a scene" as he called it. But when we docked in Calais, the Marina, wilful as ever, confounded everyone's expectations by starting like a Jaguar first time. We rolled smoothly onto foreign soil, creaking under the weight of the tents and cooking apparatus that were lashed to the roof with rope and covered by my father's army canvas.

As we moved down through France slower than Hitler's panzer divisions had done, the four of us – my parents, my older sister Lizzy and I – tried to adjust to the novel experience of being together. My mother read to me stories from Rider Haggard, Conan Doyle and John Buchan – my parents' heroes. Imprisoned in the backseat, my sister and I elbowed each other and bickered.

We entered the Grand St Bernard tunnel, still arguing, and in a foul mood. But something about the click-click of the concrete road inside the tunnel, the mesmerizing flicker of the tunnel lights and the cool alpine air on our faces lifted our spirits. It was as if someone had sucked all the friction out of the car in the darkness; we emerged into daylight feeling as if we were starting a new holiday. By the customs post, my father stretched his long legs in the Italian sunshine. He took off his cravat and changed behind the car from his trousers into a pair of long khaki shorts, left over from his days in the desert. This unconscious gesture suggested that this was a place he felt at home. This wasn't simply a holiday for him as it was for the rest of us, it was a reunion with a period of happiness in his life. He was back on Italian soil.

That night we pitched our tent on a flat piece of grass that was surrounded on three sides by a green clear river. The air was full of the calming sound of water flowing over pebbles. After we had finally finished wrestling with the rope stays and wooden pegs of my father's ancient Indian Army tent, we raced into the shallows and then cooked sausages over an open fire by the light of a Tilly lamp.

Italy was much more foreign than anything I'd ever known: the people, the taste of the tomatoes, the intensity of the sun; even the little bits of Italian history that my sister read out from her Baedeker guidebook I realised were very different from the damp clanking kings and knights of England. We meandered down through Lombardy and Tuscany. In Assisi we walked around, gasping for air in the heat. Such interest as I had in St Francis, which was never more than mild, evaporated as the leather strap of my Box Brownie cut into my neck.

"Only the English are stupid enough to walk in this," moaned my sister outside the Duomo. "The Italians are all having their siestas."

We wandered back into the coolness of the Duomo to seek relief from the scalding pavements. I longed for a gelato but knew my request would be turned down. Just then my mother announced that we were going to drive on to a place called Fontanellato.

"Where's that?" I said without enthusiasm, assuming it to be yet another medieval town. "It's where I was imprisoned in the war," said my father simply.

This was the first time that I can recall being told my father had been a prisoner of war, yet the news did not sink in immediately. Monty was still alive and it had been little more than a year since my father had taken me to see the film *Patton*; I just assumed that whatever my father had done could not compare to Monty's triumphs.

*

We stood outside the large brick building staring up. The place seemed grim and austere after the grandeur of Assisi. It had an appropriately forbidding air for a POW camp, but I was disappointed to see no sign of barbed wire or watch towers. My father knocked on the door. A small porthole opened to reveal the face of a nun in a wimple. She explained that the building was a convent. When she finally understood my father's rusty Italian, she ushered us in.

I sat on a hard bench, drinking cold lemonade provided by the nuns, watching my father and mother walk up and down the corridors. "We were given a very intensive tour by a short stout nun, Dick spreading his fingers and bending over her in his efforts at Italian," was how my mother described it in her journal. The dormitories where the POWs slept had been replaced by nuns' cells. Only the refectory in the basement was as my father remembered it.

"This was where we ate," he explained, "and where we put on plays. We put on a very good production of *Blithe Spirit* here" – a fact which seemed a little curious to me, that you could have a play in a prisoner-of-war camp.

He wanted to find the place where he had hidden his chocolate.

"Every time I received a Red Cross parcel," my father explained, "I would save the chocolate and hide it behind a loose brick in the back of one of the disused fireplaces, ready to use when I escaped. Unfortunately when I did escape everything happened so fast I didn't have time to retrieve my chocolate."

We found the room but the fireplace had been cemented over, with his chocolate inside. We wandered out of the back of the convent into a large vegetable garden. My father explained that this had once been their exercise yard – a large muddy field with a stream running through the middle. He pointed out where the barbed wire and the watchtowers had stood and showed the spot where the Italian commandant had cut the wire to let them out.

It didn't make much sense – why would the camp commandant be letting the prisoners go? I preferred to imagine Sergeant Harry Trotter of the Special Boat Squadron, one of my favourite characters in my 'war mags', wriggling under the wire as the searchlights swept the air above his head. But, nonetheless, I found myself being drawn into the story. This was a different father to the quiet somewhat reserved figure I had grown up with.

After saying goodbye to the nuns, we got back into the car and drove a short distance down a country lane.

"I think it's over there," said my father.

He stopped the car and we all got out. He strode off through a field of vines while my mother and sister stood together in the shade waiting. I trotted after him. He was clearly excited and on the verge of discovering something and I wanted to know what he was going to produce next. At the far end of the vineyard was a wood with a large dry river bed in the bottom. It was thick with brambles and saplings that criss-crossed over each other.

"Lie down there," he suggested, "and you can pretend to be me."

I burrowed under the canopy of undergrowth. Above me I could see his dim outline dressed in faded blue Airtex shirt and old army khaki shorts; his white knees unaccustomed to the light of day above a pair of long army socks held up by garters. Even by the standards of the nineteen seventies, he looked old-fashioned.

"When Vicedomini the commandant cut the wire, he told us that the Germans would soon arrive to take over the camp. We had two hours to get away. There were six hundred of us. Instead of running away as fast as we could, we decided to stick together and hide close to the camp. So we lay in this river bed as quietly as possible for two days and nights. We hoped that the Germans would never think of looking for us here. We could hear them driving around and around as they searched for us – sometimes they came down this road right past the wood but they never saw us."

"Were you scared?"

"Yes. I prayed that they would not find out where we were."

"Were there many of them?"

"Quite a few – we could see several trucks with soldiers sitting in the back and there were also motorcyclists with sidecars that raced around the roads."

"Did you have anything to eat?"

"We had a few Red Cross supplies – though not my chocolate." He chuckled. "Luckily the local people turned out to be friendly and several of the local farmers brought us cheese and milk and bread when it was dark."

I lay on the flinty soil imagining German bombers circling slowly overhead like vultures and soldiers all around me with their faces pressed down into the earth, waiting in silence, their ears picking up the engines of the motorbikes passing by only a few metres away on the dusty road.

I tried to regulate my breathing so that it could not be heard. A farmer's truck backfired in one of the fields nearby and I jumped.

"It was frightening," my father continued. "We felt very disorientated; we'd been let out of the camp but we were still in enemy territory and the Germans were moving into Italy in force to fight Monty and the Eighth Army."

"Was Monty nearby?"

"No. He had landed in Sicily in the south so he was several hundred miles away."

"What happened to the Italian commandant who let you out?"

My father glanced down at me.

"The Germans did not treat him well. He was heavily punished for what he had done. But we were always very grateful to him. The Germans never captured a single prisoner that day."

Staring up at him, I could see how proud he felt. For the first time in my life, my father began to come into focus; here was a man who had survived imprisonment and somehow escaped – not even Monty could lay claim to that.

6.

RICHARD ARRIVED AT Fontanellato prison camp on 30th May 1943. Six months had passed since he had been taken prisoner. In that time, Monty had succeeded, with the help of the Americans, in retaking the whole of North Africa. The Eighth Army had advanced two thousand miles from El Alamein to Tunis where the Germans had finally surrendered, handing over 275,000 prisoners of war.

PG49 sat on its own, just outside the town, surrounded by flat fields of vines and corn. Beyond a weak attempt at a classical façade around the front door it was void of any architectural pretence. The square block-like appearance with the rows of small windows had no doubt been intended to instil awe into the child runaways and illegitimates that it had been built to hold as an orphanage. Two 12-foot high barbed wire fences ran around the perimeter. There were a total of eight wooden watchtowers, one on each corner and one halfway down each side. Each contained two guards and a machine gun, designed so that every section of the fence was visible by a minimum of two towers. At the back of the building on the north side lay a small grass exercise area surrounded by more fences and watch towers.

The English officers were marched up the front steps into an echoing atrium which reached three stories up to the roof. Long corridors with marble floors gave off left and right, and around the top of the atrium ran a type of minstrels' gallery full of faces staring down at the new arrivals.

The Caribs' search was fairly thorough but I smuggled in everything I wanted to. We felt very much like arriving at school again for the first time. Hundreds of inquisitive people wanted to know our "dope" and all about us, and we had to learn the ways of the place. We were met by the acting Senior British Officer, Major Williams, and Adjutant Phillips and Major Pyman.

Upstairs they were shown dozens of small dormitories. There was the smell of fresh paint and Richard was relieved to see that each room had electric lighting and all the windows had glass in them. Each bed had sheets, two blankets and its own individual locker for stowing possessions.

We were told we had to divide up into rooms of six and unfortunately we didn't find it possible to do this on the spur of the moment without causing a certain amount of ill-feeling. However in the end I got in with Dennis Gibbs, Hugh Mainwaring, Peter Bragg, "Fanny" Fane-Hervey and Pop Morrison and one couldn't ask for a better lot of chaps.

Hugh Mainwaring was the officer Richard had been captured with in the desert and Fanny Fane-Hervey and Pop Morrison were both veterans from Poppi.

Out the front, facing them across the quiet tree-lined Via IV Novembre was an older, much more distinguished looking building. The Santuario Madonna del Rosario was a Dominican convent built around a wooden Madonna, whose miraculous powers were believed to have brought a dead child back to life in 1628. Behind its large baroque façade lay a huge complex of cloisters, dormitories and chapels. Every day the bells of the convent's campanile recorded the progress of the day for nuns and prisoners alike. The nuns washed the clothes of the prisoners in return for receiving scarce necessities like soap from the Red Cross parcels. Occasionally the prisoners would glimpse the nuns in the windows of the convent and from time to time, a prisoner would find a little note hidden inside their clothes bestowing the blessings of the Madonna del Rosario on the wearer. They discovered that they were in Northern Italy, between Parma and Milan.

"We're less than 200 kilometres from the Swiss border," someone noted hopefully. Only one POW had ever been taken to the local town of Fontanellato; he reported seeing farmers' stalls set up in the arches at the foot of the huge castle of Rocca Sanvitale, and a memorial to those who had died in the First World War with a surprisingly long list of names of the dead.

The total number in PG49 was 500 officers and 100 Other Ranks. There was a roll call at around 7am which sometimes took over an hour to complete, and another in the evening. In between, the day was largely their own. "We settled down slowly, not liking the rowdy jostling life after our quiet retreat at Poppi."

But Poppi had at least acclimatised him to life in prison. Richard could immediately recognise the ones who had come straight from the front. They wandered the corridors with a dazed expression, still living in the frenetic shock of battle, unable to focus on the present. The emptiness of the days was a form of a torture for many of them. Life in prison was like an interminable Saturday afternoon, said one prisoner, each dusty hour marked by the bells of the convent campanile. The newly captured found it hard to cope with the abrupt decline in their status from being in the privileged position of an officer in Britain's imperial army to a prisoner with no command over anything.

No one had any idea when the war was going to end and no control over its course; they had a nagging sense that they had "let the side down". The war was still raging all around but they were no longer a part of it - it was hard not to feel a failure in some way and the gung-ho language of the camp often masked depression. On bad nights, the dormitories echoed with the muffled screams of men reliving their battles. There was the rear gunner who seemed condemned to return to his bale-out in his dreams. Night after night he relived the sight of his co-pilot falling past him without a parachute, his face contorted in panic. Then there was the sub-mariner, whose vessel had been hit by a German torpedo and who had been the last man to make it out of the emergency hatch, leaving his companions to drown in the dark, oily water that sleuced greedily through the opening.

On one of his first mornings in the exercise yard, Richard watched two figures walking around pulling pieces of wood on strings behind them, occasionally pausing to talk to each other.

"You entered *Prancer* for that show up in Cheltenham last weekend," said one. "I heard the prize money was pretty decent…"

"Tried to, but the judges ruled that he was too old."

"How could they say that? Seems the symbol of virility to me. What is he? A poodle/lab cross?"

Richard watched the two men stare down at the piece of wood with *Prancer* painted on the top.

"No, all poodle. Won every cup south of the Thames in his day."

There was a strange array of clothing on display in the exercise yard, everyone doing their best to defy the ban on civilian clothes. Those who had been inside the longest had woollen scarves and pullovers and even civilian trousers that had been shipped to them from England before the ban came in. Some prisoners who had been shot down or captured at sea had arrived at camp without any uniform, and had cobbled together an eccentric array of night gowns, old farming clothes, and army uniform. The only unifying

PG49, converted from an old orphanage, at Fontanellato

feature was the red patch of cloth that everyone had to have sewn onto their backs to show that they were prisoners.

*

Contact with home was patchy. Richard was allowed to send one letter a month. A reply would take two or three months. Sometimes, he would get five or six letters at once for no good reason. Occasionally, a prisoner would receive a letter from someone who was dead, like the light from a distant star that has since vanished. Richard always made a point of asking for books. Since the camp had only been in existence for six months, the prison library was small. And every book was censored by both the British and the Italians; the British wanted to make sure that nothing was being sent that might help the enemy, and the Italian guards tore off the front and back covers in case they hid a map or some other aid for escaping.

The POWs believed, because of the Italian army's weak performance in the desert that somehow the Italians would be ineffectual prison wardens. But in fact, the *carabinieri* and *Alpini* soldiers who guarded Italian POW camps were considerably more efficient at their job than their German counterparts. There were fewer successful escapes from POW camps in Italy than from those in Nazi Germany and of the POWs who did get out, very few made it home. Of the 602 escape attempts recorded in Italy before the Armistice was signed, only six individuals are known to have managed a "home run" all the way back to the UK.

Moreover, the Italians managed to guard their prisoners without resorting to the systematic brutality that was endemic in German camps. At PG49, Richard soon realised that they were particularly fortunate to have Colonello Vicedomini as their commandant. Eugenio Vicedomini had fought alongside the British in the First World War when Italy and Britain had been on the same side against Germany. Like many career officers in Mussolini's army, he regarded Italy's alliance with Hitler and the Nazis as a disaster for his country. Guarding prisoners was a job that enabled him to maintain his allegiance to the army that he had sworn to serve without compromising his integrity. He conducted himself with humanity and compassion.

One day, a prisoner had seized a fleeting opportunity to escape and had managed to get out of the camp only to be stopped by a *carabiniere* who stepped out unexpectedly from behind a tree. In less than ten minutes the POW was back inside the camp in Vicedomini's office. If anything was likely to enrage a camp commandant, it was an escape attempt, but Vicedomini showed no anger, only concern.

"*Tenente* Comyn," said the elderly Colonello to the POW. "My sentries on the wire might have shot you. And then what would your mother have said?"

Lieutenant Comyn was so surprised by the commandant's reaction, he had no reply. He was given the minimum punishment of 28 days in solitary. But such stories of compassion only seemed to irritate some prisoners. They were furious at being POWs which

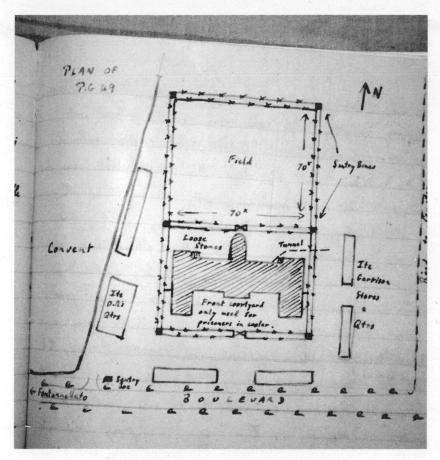

**The layout of the camp at Fontanellato,
drawn by Richard in his notebook**

they saw as a badge of shame and they took it out on the guards, trying to provoke them into more extreme responses which might somehow atone for the humiliation of being held captive. Vicedomini would not be drawn in, however, and persisted in treating the British officers more like equals than prisoners.

He arranged for every prisoner to receive two glasses of wine a day. At midday in time for lunch, the guards delivered an aperitif of vermouth and in the early evening they handed out a ration of the local *vino lavorato* to accompany their dinner. Keen to have some control over the distribution of alcohol among the men, the

Senior British Officer Colonel de Burgh asked the Italians not to give the wine out individually. Instead he invited a gregarious RAF pilot called Tommy Pitman to establish a POW bar on the minstrel's gallery that ran along the top of the atrium where the camp allocation of wine was delivered every day.

In lieu of their daily wine ration, each prisoner was given a 'chit' which they could cash in at the bar. Since the wine was pretty much a constant, the chits quickly became a form of camp currency which could be used to purchase other rarer commodities like chocolate or cigarettes. The more abstemious you were the richer you became.

"Tommy's Bar" was open for two hours at lunchtime and two hours in the evening. On one side of the bar the prisoners would lean over the banisters and jeer at their friends in the entrance hall twenty feet below, sometimes throwing down the empty ration tins

Corner of Field.

**A drawing of the exercise field at Fontanellato,
from Richard's notebook**

that were used as wine glasses onto the heads of the passers-by like schoolboys. On the other side of the bar they would lounge against the windows and look out into the street. As the weather improved, the girls of Fontanellato began to take their evening *passeggiata* on the road. With their men either conscripted into the army or in hiding dodging the conscription, the girls gravitated towards the POW camp as one of the few places where they could flirt, albeit at long range. Showing off their brown legs beneath cotton farm dresses, they would stroll slowly past the camp fence, as if on a catwalk, arm in arm either with each other or with their mothers or grandmothers. The guards in the watchtowers would turn their backs on the camp to talk to them while behind them the occupants of Tommy's Bar looked on from a distance.

It wasn't usually long before one of the prisoners, fired up by the vino lavorato, would yell a crude invitation. The NCO in charge of the guards, under pressure to defend his womenfolk from slander, would scream at his men who would turn around and loose off several rounds in the direction of the windows. This would provoke more taunts and insults from the prisoners and in turn more shots. Sometimes a prisoner who felt a bullet singe his ear would go too far and yell something about the NCO's mother, and then an order would be yelled in the guardroom below followed by the crash of boots up the marble stairs. Tommy would be told to close up the bar and the Italians would retreat, grumbling about how the British couldn't handle their drink.

Like any new boy, Richard worked hard to learn the traditions of PG49. Once he'd got over the shock of how big it was compared to Poppi, he realised that being in a larger camp had several advantages. Here was a chance to spend one's day immersed in ancient Rome, or learning Italian, playing bridge or simply sunbathing in the deckchairs at the end of the exercise field. He joined in the sporting competitions in the exercise yard. The rugby seven-a-side was dominated by the South Africans who beat all-comers. The football league which Richard took part in carried betting on the side, organised by an indefatigable RAF pilot called Bill Rainford, known to everyone as Rainy.

Marcus the dentist held his surgeries on the touchline, hoping the games would provide some mildly distracting anaesthetic for the patient as his teeth were wrenched out with primitive pliers and without painkillers. A small muddy stream ran through the middle of the exercise yard which was home to four fluffy goslings stolen from a nearby pond by one of the guards. When a game was on, they liked to run in and out of the legs of the players, scuttling back to safety when it got too rough.

Richard discovered that Rainy, who had been shot down in a Blenheim bomber on the first day of the war, also ran something called "Opportunities Ltd." which claimed to offer "every service except escape". For a fee, Rainy would procure additional cigarettes and chocolate for his clients, find someone to do another officer's duty in the kitchens, rescue dropped objects from the dark scuttling rat colonies in the *gabinetti*, procure front row seats for popular shows and run errands. Another business was "Rack and Ruin", which offered a mending and repair service, was run by Jack Clarke, a quiet engineer from the Midlands.

*

As Richard found his feet, he began to enjoy the camp life. To anyone who'd grown up in an all male boarding school the routines and the tribalism of PG49 were very familiar. Richard noticed that there was a clique of Old Etonians and Harrovians, who had as little contact as possible with the rest of the camp – a motley collection of minor aristocrats, gentlemen soldiers, amateur jockeys and sons of lairds who were apparently just filling in the time until they inherited their titles. He was both fascinated and horrified by the air of mild indifference and bemusement with which they viewed the fortunes of war, as if it was someone else's game in which they had been invited to play as guests. They were never to be found crowded around the secret radio listening for the BBC, unless there was a chance it might carry some snippet about some 'scrape' that one of their own was involved in.

They moved together as a single herd and spoke a language almost unintelligible to anyone else, sprinkled with names and references to incidents and connections that only members of their class would understand: what Randolph Churchill's fag at Eton was called, how Claude Lascelles had lost the tip of his little finger, what happened during the hunting party of '24 on the Duke of Buccleuch's Yorkshire estate and the incident at Asprey's that led to the Montagu-Tessington affair.

The only thing they seemed to take seriously was the shallow gene pool in which their families had swum for generations, governed by codes that had outlasted many previous wars and disturbances. They acknowledged other prisoners only if one of their clan needed something that could increase their comfort, and then they purchased or charmed their way to possession. Even the camp's Senior British Officer, Colonel Hugh de Burgh, was excluded from their ranks because he was an Artillery officer without an estate or title to his name.

After dinner each night, those that belonged to White's Club in London met in the basement to play baccarat for sizeable stakes that they honoured by signing instructions that were sent on to their banks in St James's. They opened books on running races between prisoners. Each "owner" would train his stable of runners, feeding them extra rations at mealtimes and timing them on the gallops round the exercise yard imagining they were with their beloved racehorses back at Newmarket.

One day Eric Newby, the author, running in one of the races, miscalculated the number of laps and slowed down, thinking he had finished. A disappointed White's Club member approached him afterwards, "You didn't pull the race, Eric, did you?" he asked. Newby looked at him, bemused. He had no idea how much was at stake.

Richard was delighted to discover there was a flourishing

Drama Group and he revelled in the opportunity to dress up, and to take off the uniform which he had worn continuously since university. The group's repertoire was limited by what the players could get hold of. Besides *Blithe Spirit*, Richard took part in Shaw's *Pygmalion* and a weak attempt at Somerset Maugham's *The Circle*. Each show was treated with the ceremony of an opening night: the Senior British Officer, Colonel de Burgh, would walk in with his staff and take his place like the Royal Party on the only line of chairs at the front, while everyone else sat on upturned Red Cross boxes behind.

Once a week Colonello Vicedomini allowed all prisoners not in solitary confinement to go on escorted walks through the countryside. They would march out at 7am before the heat of the day set in, 120 at a time flanked by their carabinieri guards. It seems remarkable that no one attempted to escape during these excursions - perhaps for fear of jeopardising the treat for others. This walk was one of the greatest privileges imaginable for a prisoner, a chance to re-establish contact with the outside world and let the senses break out of the unchanging scenes and smells that surrounded them 24 hours a day. They marched in boisterous formation three abreast through the poplar-lined lanes, inhaling the smells from barns full of ripening wheels of parmesan, and staring at farmyards of pigs and chickens and fields of sugar beet and vines. Italians were told to stay out of sight when the prisoners went past.

Once, a group of prisoners increased the pace to try to out-march the guards. Soon they were marching 140 paces to the minute and the guards were screaming at them to halt. After that the marches were conducted at a funereal pace for several weeks as punishment but to Richard's relief they weren't stopped.

The greatest hardship at the camp was malnutrition and a permanent feeling of hunger. Everyone at Fontanellato was supposed to receive one Red Cross parcel a week consisting of tins of biscuits, cheese, chocolate, jam, oats, dried eggs and meat. One of the prisoners, a Belgian lieutenant called Leon Blanchaert, was a talented cook, so instead of distributing the Red Cross food parcels individually it was decided that all food parcels should be pooled and handed over to the kitchens under Blanchaert's supervision.

Lieutenant Blanchaert did his best to make the meals interesting and filling but there was never enough and almost as soon as each meal ended, the hunger would return. The thought of food crowded out every other appetite including sex. However in summer, the Italians provided a bit more fresh fruit and vegetables which raised the vitamin levels and revived the men's interest in sex. Since the village girls were out of reach, the only options were sex between prisoners or masturbation. Each night there would be a few furtive attempts at masturbating under the bedcovers. Through the un-curtained windows, the searchlights from the watchtowers would graze the beds, catching the undulating blankets in a white stage light.

Under British law homosexuality was illegal and was even more heavily demonised within the army since it was widely believed to sap the fighting spirit. The only known account of a gay love affair in a Second World War British POW camp was actually written by two prisoners who fell in love in PG49. Though nominally a work of fiction, "The Cage" by Dan Billany and David Dowie, describes Fontanellato in great detail including the walks in the country, Tommy's Bar and Bill Rainsford's "Opportunities Ltd".

Most of the book is an account of the unrequited love that "Alan" feels for the much more glamorous "David". Every evening Alan stands in the bar leaning over the balustrade watching David playing cards below:

"Looking down into the hall from the balcony I can see the table, the four heads, the cards, and a glass of vino by each hand. Quietness, steadiness, mutual understanding. Cigarette-smoke floating. Interest and humour on their faces, looking at their cards and at each other. The lamp-light on his gold-brown hair. Heedless. Touch his hair with the invisible shaft of my glance. The only contact. Back now and lie flat on my bed, beside his empty bed. Press my locked hands tight over my eyes. But I can't shut my thoughts out…"

"The Cage" gives a good sense of the claustrophobia of prison camp, where privacy was a rare commodity and where every phrase was magnified by the close proximity of existence. "If we wanted to talk privately, it meant crawling away to some less frequented corner and leaning out of a window, and these elaborate arrangements somehow destroyed the whole pleasure of a conversation."

Dan Billany and David Dowie escaped together from Fontanellato, but never made it home. The last time they were seen was about 70 miles from the Allied lines high in the Apennine mountains. They died, apparently together, in unknown circumstances as winter approached.

One day three years after the war had ended, a package arrived at the small house in Somerset where Dan Billany's parents lived. It contained the manuscript for "The Cage" with a note from an Italian farmer called Meletti saying that Dan and David had stayed with him for a few nights while they were on the run and entrusted him with the manuscript. They asked him to post it to England if they never came back to reclaim it.

*

One evening not long after he'd arrived in the camp, Richard was surprised to come across a childhood friend in the bar. Carol Mather had grown up not far from Richard's grandparents in Cheshire. Through his friendship with the family, Mather had met Monty and had made enough of an impression to be able to secure a place on Monty's staff in the desert. It was Carol Mather whom Monty had sent out to bring home his errant general Lumsden. Mather always gave the impression of being on the inside of anything that was happening. In his memoir of wartime experiences that he wrote 50 years later called "When the Grass Stops

Growing", he portrayed the war as a spirited romp full of midnight raids, nights dressing up as Arabs, and playing poker onboard Navy ships before a commando landing. He briefly belonged to Stirling's Long Range Desert Patrol, the forerunner of the SAS.

As Mather boasted about his achievements in the desert at Tommy's Bar, Richard felt rather self-conscious of his capture after less than a month in the front line. The only justifiable activity in POW camp, Mather said, was to try to escape. He poured scorn on the sports competitions, the Oscar Wilde performances, the lectures on Italian art and archaeology and the earnest attempts to recreate an officers' mess in an orphanage in northern Italy.

"It's all madness," Mather proclaimed as he knocked back his wine from the tin cup. "Madness. They're just lotus-eaters."

Richard did not mention his membership of the drama society. He could see why Monty approved of this action man; he was exactly the kind of can-do officer that Monty liked to have around.

"I have an idea for an escape," said Mather leaning closer. "but I need your help. I'm convinced that we can dig a tunnel from underneath the front steps. There's a ventilation grill in the wall of the dining room that leads under the steps where there's a large space." Richard was one of the most senior Royal Engineer officers in the camp and Mather needed Richard's engineering expertise to design the tunnel and to make sure it was strong enough because it would be passing underneath the front yard where vehicles went in and out. Richard said he would be happy to help.

That evening after the final roll call, the two of them inspected the space under the steps and found it was almost big enough to stand in. Richard could see it offered an ideal location to start a tunnel; they could hide tools in there and even store some of the earth that they removed. However, after assessing the site further, he told Mather that the plan was unworkable. "I turned it down as being too difficult owing to the high water level," he explained in his diary. It's possible that Richard's urge to escape had waned.

The news from the desert was continuing to improve. Why risk everything on a break-out when he might be free in a few weeks?

Surprised and perhaps a bit annoyed, Mather brushed aside Richard's objections and went ahead anyway. To avoid the high water table and yet allow enough soil above to make it strong enough to support a vehicle, the tunnel could only be 18 inches tall. Mather and his team set to work right away. Each night after the evening roll call was over, the guards would lock the doors of the orphanage and withdraw to their positions on the watchtowers. This gave the prisoners all night until the morning roll call at 7am to dig. Inside the crawl space under the steps, Mather and his colleagues rigged up an electric light, running the cable from a socket in the dining room, and built a flue from Red Cross tins with a bellows at one end, which pumped fresh air down to where they were digging.

Some of their equipment they received from MI9, the arm of British Military Intelligence responsible for helping Allied personnel stuck behind enemy lines to get home. The staff of MI9 consisted of a number of eccentrics including a former magician called Jasper Maskelyne who conjured up devices to assist British POWs to escape: baseball bats and cricket bats that contained saws and collapsible shovels, forged identity papers, maps inside playing cards and board games full of real money.

To get this equipment into the POW camps, MI9 set up fake charities with innocuous sounding names like the Welsh Provident Society and the Lancashire Penny Fund and sent letters, apparently written by an elderly widow or a country vicar, asking for their "parcels of cheer" to be distributed to British prisoners. According to MI9's records, they successfully dispatched 9,247 maps, 1,119 hacksaws, 427 sets of dyes and 297 blankets that could be used to make civilian clothes.

Work on the tunnel had been going for about two months when one night a guard patrolling outside spotted the light through a tiny crack in the front steps. The prisoners had just enough time to get out before the guards rushed into the basement, pulled off the grill and found the digging equipment. "The tunnel deserved a better fate," Richard wrote, "but I'm sorry to say that it was discovered after a progress of only about fifteen feet." Mather and his accomplices did not admit to the crime so the entire camp was punished by having all walks in the countryside cancelled for a month. The Italians then made the POWs dig a deep ditch between the two fences so that any further tunnels would be exposed.

*

On the morning of Sunday July 25th 1943 as summer reached its height, Richard lay in a deckchair with one of his beloved Trollope novels. He was gazing through the wire at the Italian farm workers in the vineyards, when he suddenly heard shouts coming from inside the building where the early occupants of Tommy's Bar had been startled by a commotion in the guards' accommodation outside. Rushing to the windows, they watched off-duty guards stream out of the huts, most of them wearing only shirts and trousers and no jackets. They began dancing in the road, grabbing anyone who happened to be walking by. At first, the prisoners thought the Italians were celebrating the victory of the local football team, but then, to their astonishment, the guards started to rip down posters of Mussolini from the walls of the convent and stamp them underfoot.

Somewhere in the camp Richard knew that a radio was hidden; its exact location was a closely guarded secret but everyone benefited from its presence. It had taken four months to assemble in secret using stray pieces of metal and wire from the theatrical props department. The only piece they could not make themselves, the radio valve, had been provided by a corrupt guard in exchange for a large amount of chocolate and cash. And when the atmospherics were right, it worked well enough to be able to pick up the BBC Home Service.

An American journalist called Larry Allen who had been

plucked from the sea off Tobruk would tune in each day and write a daily summary of news which he posted every morning on a noticeboard outside Tommy's Bar. By carefully weaving information from the BBC into the digest of dry Italian government pronouncements he was able to avoid alerting the authorities to the radio's presence. On 25th July, he posted a bulletin which read simply, "Flash. Benito finito!"

The news spread rapidly through the camp: Mussolini had been deposed. Some thought it meant the end of the war and expected the guards to fling open the gates of the camp at once. Rainy immediately opened a book on how long it would take for the Allies to liberate the camp. The optimists, talking wildly of amphibious landings in Genoa, bet on a week. But others were less sanguine and noticed that, after their celebrations, the guards went back to their positions in the watch towers. Mussolini may have gone, but Italy had not surrendered. It was still an enemy, albeit a fairly reluctant one.

Among his papers after his death, I found one letter from my father written to his beloved Aunt Bulley from inside the camp at the time. Prisoners' letters comprised one piece of paper without an envelope or glue which was folded inside itself. This was to allow censors at every stage to read it without difficulty. "*Posta di prigioniero di guerra*," it says on the outside and above that my father wrote, "*via Aerea Roma-Lisbona-Londra*", as if helping to guide the flimsy airmail letter across the battlefields of Europe to the house at the end of the gravel drive outside Hindhead where Aunt Bulley tended to her rhododendrons.

It was written on July 30th 1943 – five days after the news of Mussolini's arrest had broken. "The news seems so good that one wonders whether it is worth writing. In fact I suppose you will only get this if we have been disappointed in our hopes. The paper has been very exciting reading the last few days. Camp life goes on much the same except that walks are temporarily suspended. I told you in my last p.c. that the parcel of books containing the

Bible and the book on architecture had arrived back from the censors. I like the latter, it is not the same as any already in our library and has a lot in it without being frightfully technical. They all had their backs torn off them and I have rebound the Bible myself with cloth.

"I also had a parcel last week of drawing things from Winsor & Newton. Please thank whoever sent it. I think it may have been Mrs Reynolds if it wasn't your good selves. Lastly I had a book from the Bodleian, the only one I have received to date. It has been very hot here recently, not of course comparable to India as I often remind my room companions to their great annoyance; but still hot and there are a good many mosquitoes about. One longs for a bathe, but we are lucky to have good cold baths. Love from Dick."

*

The coup against Mussolini had been building for some time. So long as the war had been going the Axis way, Mussolini had been safe. But as Monty advanced closer and closer to Italy, the pressure on Il Duce grew. On July 10th, Monty landed in Sicily. Within a week, General Patton had captured Palermo and both he and Monty were heading for the Straits of Messina. It was obvious that an Allied invasion of the Italian mainland was imminent. A cabal of Mussolini's advisors decided that Il Duce had to be removed for the sake of Italy. On July 24th 1943 at a meeting of Mussolini's cabinet, they called on the cabinet to remove Mussolini and restore power to the king. The plotters, knowing the risk of opposing Il Duce so openly, had packed hand grenades into their briefcases in case he ordered their arrest. The motion passed, but Mussolini left the room assuming that they were bluffing.

The next morning, however, to Mussolini's astonishment, King Victor Emmanuel informed him that in the light of the cabinet's decision, he had invited Marshal Pietro Badoglio to form a new government.

Badoglio was an old First World War general who had led

the invasion of Ethiopia in the 1930s and had been given the title of the Duke of Addis Ababa by Mussolini as a reward. Mussolini walked out of the King's palace stunned that they could think of replacing him with such a docile fool. When he got outside he found that his car had disappeared; in its place stood a Red Cross ambulance which he was ordered to get into. He was driven to a police barracks in the centre of Rome. On the orders of the King, carabinieri quickly surrounded the Fascist party headquarters to prevent a counter-coup. None came. It was a Sunday afternoon and Mussolini was finished.

That evening at Frascati, a few miles outside Rome, Field Marshal Kesselring, the commander of German forces in Italy, was having dinner when a messenger brought the news that Mussolini had been removed from power. The much vaunted German intelligence had not picked up the possibility of a coup. Kesselring was alarmed; the Third Reich had a only two and a half divisions on the Italian mainland with a further four fighting the Allies in Sicily.

Hitler's first reaction was to send Kesselring to Rome to arrest Badoglio and restore Mussolini – the problem was no one knew where Mussolini was. Instead, General Kesselring suggested feigning support for Badoglio to keep him from going over to the Allies. He called the general and asked how many German divisions he needed to protect Italy. When Badoglio vacillated, saying it was not his decision, Kesselring interpreted it as carte blanche to bring in as many as he could. Had Badoglio acted decisively he could have closed the Brenner Pass between Italy and Austria and prevented any German reinforcements from entering the country. But the 72-year-old general was incapable of acting swiftly. For 21 years, Mussolini had made every important decision relating to military matters and the general, like most of the cabinet, had lost the habit of making decisions himself. The old lion of Addis was grieving the loss of a son and his wife and was said to be drinking heavily.

Within two weeks of Mussolini's arrest, the Germans had

moved six newly equipped divisions into Italy. At Fontanellato, Richard stood beside the wire with the others and watched in dismay as unit after unit of well-armed German soldiers drove past. "Quite a lot came by our camp and bivouacked in a neighbouring field," Richard wrote in his diary in early August.

> *The wishful-thinkers among us wanted to make out that they were on their way north, evacuating the country. But it was obvious that there were fresh troops, very young most of them with new equipment and it seemed to me only natural that they were on their way to La Spezia and Rome and possibly further south where the Germans must be expecting landings. They marched down the road looking very fit and whenever they passed our camp they always struck up one of their militaristic songs. The Italians kept well out of their way.*

7.

RICHARD'S DISMAY AT watching the Germans streaming down the roads of Italy was shared by 80,000 other British POWs who were imprisoned in Italian camps that summer. For some time MI9 had been debating within itself what to do in the event that Italy pulled out of the war. It was MI9's job to help POWs. But what advice should it give to them? Should it urge them to stay in the camps or try to escape? And once out, should they be told to join the resistance or try to find their way home? In MI9's short existence it had never encountered the predicament of how to handle thousands of POWs at once.

· The head of MI9, Brigadier Norman Crockatt, who had been in charge of the London Stock Exchange before the war, instinctively disliked the prospect of mass breakouts. He believed that it would cause chaos on the battlefield and might precipitate reprisals by parts of the Italian army who did not support the surrender. Furthermore, he considered the malnourished POWs to be of little value as fighting soldiers.

Crockatt and his team concluded that Monty would sweep up

Italy in a matter of a few days anyway. Under this scenario, they believed, the best alternative was to tell the POWs to "stay put" and wait in their camps for the Allied forces to arrive.

At Allied Forces Headquarters in Algiers, MI9's views were greeted with astonishment; the Italians might surrender but no one believed that the Germans were going to walk away from Italy and allow the Allies to march up to the Alps unopposed. It could be weeks, they argued, before Allied forces reached the camps – and the Germans, who were already in Italy, would almost certainly get there before them. Even MI9's own officer in the Middle East, Colonel Simonds, realised the madness of the order and tried to argue against it.

But on 7th June 1943, MI9 in London issued Order P/W 87190: "…in the event of an Allied invasion of Italy, officers commanding prison camps will ensure that prisoners-of-war remain within camp. Authority is granted to all officers commanding to take necessary disciplinary action to prevent individual prisoners-of-war attempting to rejoin their own units."

To get the message to the Senior British Officers in the camps, MI9 used an ingenious method. MI9 knew that many of the camps had built clandestine radios in order to listen to the BBC. One of the most famous figures on the BBC was the "Radio Padre", the Reverend Selby Wright, who broadcast a weekly talk every Wednesday evening at 7pm to British forces around the world. Thanks to Wright's simple unpatronising manner, the Radio Padre was the second most popular show on the BBC after Tommy Handley the comedian.

Selby Wright received 1,000 fan letters a day, but he didn't like the limelight and was keen to return to being an ordinary military chaplain in the field. In September 1942, he had finally obtained permission to step away from the microphone. But MI9 had other ideas and he was ordered to return, this time with an additional mission.

Over the next six months, MI9 inserted a series of messages using a secret code known as HK into the text of the padre's talk, being careful not to tamper too much with the meaning. The means of deciphering the HK code had been distributed to the camps on silk handkerchiefs hidden inside cans of food. HK was not particularly complex but it appears that the Germans and Italians never broke it.

The Reverend Wright had no idea what the messages were, only that his talk had been "adjusted". Each time this happened, he was told to open his talk with the words "Good Evening, Forces" instead of "Hello" or just "Good Evening" – this was the signal for any POWs listening on their radios that there was a message for them hidden between the lines of Christian reassurance.

During June and July 1943 MI9 broadcast the "stay put" order to POW camps all over Italy. MI9's official history states proudly, "It is a tribute to the efficiency [MI9] had attained that almost every camp's SBO received the message in time." Brigadier Crockatt, the head of MI9, "was happy at what was being done".

Later, when the full disaster of what had been done became clear, MI9 tried to blame the order on Monty, claiming that he "probably gave his directive… in late May or early June when nominally on leave in London." But the original order has disappeared from the archives – its existence known only from references to it in other communications – so the truth of who actually instigated the notorious "stay put" order may never be known.

In Fontanellato, MI9's message was duly decoded and passed on to Colonel Hugh de Burgh, the camp's Senior British Officer. At first it did not seem an unreasonable order and even added slightly to the sense of optimism. But as summer wore on, and the POWs watched unit after unit of German soldiers marching down the road towards the front, the mood changed. It became obvious to everyone that, despite Mussolini's departure, the Germans were going to stand and fight in Italy. For camps like Fontanellato located in the north of Italy far from the Allies and well inside the area of German control, the "stay put" order seemed like an invitation to become a prisoner of the Germans.

One afternoon in late August, the POWs in the yard were shaken from their torpor by the unaccustomed sound of propellers. A few of them started squinting upwards and then waving and pointing; others joined in and soon hundreds of prisoners were whooping with delight as they watched forty American Flying Fortress bombers drone slowly through the blue sky, the sunlight glinting off their fuselages. It was the POWs' first sighting of the Allies in Italy.

Just then there was a whump whump – as an anti-aircraft battery opened up nearby – and the whoops turned to jeers and curses.

"You couldn't hit a plane if it landed on top of you!" someone yelled at the Italian gunners, positioned on the edge of the field about a quarter of a mile away.

Then to everyone's astonishment including the Italian guards, smoke began to belch from one of the bombers' tails and three tiny white dots slowly separated themselves from the smoke and began to fall towards earth. The prisoners rushed to the fence to watch. The parachutists floated to the east, disappearing out of sight on the other side of the town. A few seconds later there was a whistling sound and a piece of twisted American bomber fuselage - made somewhere in the plains of Kansas - smashed into a row of vines just beside the anti-aircraft battery, causing the Italian gunners to cry out in alarm.

Guards clambered onto the camp truck and disappeared in a clatter of dust down the road in the direction of the parachutes. Half an hour later, the truck returned. The habitués of Tommy's bar leaned out of the window and yelled questions at the dazed crew as they were pushed quickly into the guardroom. To everyone's frustration they were kept in a separate location from the camp so no one had the chance to talk to them and find out how the war was progressing.

*

On 3rd September 1943, Monty crossed the Straits of Messina from Sicily and landed on the Italian mainland.

"My dear Brookie", he wrote to the Chief of the Imperial General Staff, Field Marshal Alan Brooke, "I attacked across the straits of Messina this morning at 0430. At 1030 I stepped ashore myself on the mainland of Europe just north of Reggio. It was a great thrill once more to set foot on the Continent from which we were pushed off three years ago at Dunkirk! The Germans evacuated Reggio before we got into town so we had no opposition there from soldiers, but there is a zoo in the town and our shelling broke open some cages; a puma and a monkey escaped and attacked some men of the HQ 3rd Canadian brigade. I have enjoyed it all greatly."

That same day at Fairfield Camp in Sicily, the Italians signed an Armistice with the Allied Forces; Italy was out of the war but its status remained unclear. No order was given to the Italian soldiers to fight the Germans, King Victor Emmanuel told them only not to resist the Allies. As soon as this was issued, General Badoglio, the King and the most of the government fled Rome; within 24 hours, the Italian War Office was empty, leaving junior officers to answer the phone calls from bewildered unit commanders all over Italy asking what they should do. On 11th September, the Italian War Office finally sent out a message from the safety of Brindisi ordering all Italian soldiers to treat the Germans as enemy, but it was too late.

The Germans moved quickly. They swept through central Italy rounding up the confused units; they treated their erstwhile allies as enemies, showing them little mercy. Many were shot on the spot or sent to German POW camps in cattle trains. General Kesselring boasted to Hitler that within four days 700,000 Italian soldiers had been captured along with 56 divisions' worth of equipment and material. All of Italy from Rome northwards was placed under

German martial law and treated as an occupied country. German military currency replaced the lira. Italy may have surrendered but the battle for control of Italy had only just begun.

In the six-week hiatus between the coup against Mussolini and Italy's final surrender, as British Intelligence described German divisions pouring across the Alps into Italy, MI9 had plenty of opportunity to rescind Order P/W 87190 and transmit fresh instructions via the Radio Padre. But it didn't.

Churchill and the War Cabinet remained unaware of what MI9 had done. In the negotiations that took place that summer with the Italian government, Churchill had insisted that the Italian War Ministry release all British POWs at the earliest opportunity. Article 3 of the Armistice that was signed in Sicily that September stated: "All prisoners or internees of the United Nations to be immediately turned over to the Allied Commander in Chief and none of these may now or at any time be evacuated to Germany."

As soon as the Armistice was signed, the Italian War Ministry ordered all camp commandants to release British prisoners under their control, but in the confusion of those final days, some commandants did not receive the order. Others chose to ignore it; after years of holding men in captivity, it hurt their professional pride simply to open the gate and turn their prisoners loose. A few even made preparations to defend their camps against the Germans while others decided to hand over the camps intact to the German occupiers.

At PG5, the "Italian Colditz", as it was known, near Gavi in the Piedmont, the Italian commandant refused to open the gates when the Armistice was declared, despite a ferocious argument with the Senior British Officer. When the Germans arrived the next day the entire camp was handed over to them. Realising what was happening, some of the prisoners tried to hide inside the camp but were quickly found. 800 men were put on cattle trains and shunted north to Germany.

Further north at PG57 near Trieste, the commandant withdrew his guards, but the Senior British Officer, loyal to the 'stay put' order, kept the gates closed and ordered the prisoners not to leave. Within 24 hours the camp was surrounded by Germans and the window of opportunity had closed.

When the Italian guards abandoned PG21 in Chieti in the middle of the night, and the SBO Colonel Marshall threatened to court-martial any POW who left the camp, there was a near mutiny among the prisoners. He appointed his own phalanx of guards and ordered them to man the watchtowers. In the end, many of the prisoners could not bring themselves to disobey a high ranking officer and for a week remained docilely where they were – guarded by British guards in an Italian POW camp. When a battalion of German paratroopers arrived they were astonished to discover prisoners still milling around inside the camp compound, with no sign of Italian guards. The entire camp population – about 1300 soldiers – was shipped by train to the Nazi camps in Poland and Germany.

At Allied Headquarters in Algiers, the implications of MI9's order began to sink in. Colonel Simonds, the lone voice of MI9 who had protested the order, was summoned urgently and told to do whatever he could to rescue as many POWs as possible. He was given the use of several boats and allowed to request air sorties. He hastily assembled a small group to organise escape paths for POWs through German lines.

But for most of the prisoners it was too late.

Out of the 80,000 British POWs in Italy at the time of the Armistice, 50,000 – more than half – were immediately captured by the Germans and shipped north. Of those who did escape, only 11,500 made it all the way home: 5,000 by crossing the Alps into Switzerland and 6,500 by reaching the Allied forces coming up Italy.

The rest were either rounded up or shot by the Germans on the run or just faded into the countryside, settling in the mountain villages of the Apennines and never going home. Some 2,000 were never accounted for.

What happened at Fontanellato was unique.

8.

SOME SIXTY YEARS later, my father and I sit side by side in his little car overlooking the Solent, as a blustery wind sends patinas of seawater and rain sliding down the windscreen. He is now 92. Though increasingly frail he stubbornly refuses to entertain the idea of moving to a nursing home. I live in America and worry about him a lot. I fly over as often as I can, but mostly it is only for three or four days, just long enough to conquer the jet lag before heading back to my own family.

He is dozing in the driver's seat with a copy of *The Times* propped against the steering wheel, folded to the letters to the editor. He's ticked the letters he's read with a black and red HB pencil stub that he always carries in his pocket.

As I study the faint outline of the Isle of Wight across the Solent I try to calculate how many hours he has been alive. He was born in May 1914, three months before the First World War began. 92 years is approximately 800,000 hours. His heart has beaten every second of every day since then – nearly 3 billion times.

A seagull belly-flops onto the car roof causing my father to open his eyes. He studies the drizzle for a couple of seconds then turns and notices me sitting beside him as if for the first time. He blinks, his bright blue eyes like small pools under the craggy outcrops of his eyebrows. "What have you been thinking?" he asks.

"I was trying to calculate how many hours you've lived."

He chuckles, coughs and chuckles again.

"Oh my goodness. Far too many I should think."

That evening after my father has gone to bed, I sit in his study, amidst the piles of his watercolours and old files, and examine the tiny green diary once more, the one that he had pulled out of a box of papers from under his desk ten years earlier. I read a few pages and turn the compass around in my hand, marveling at the way the safety pin still faithfully swings around to find the North. It strikes me how he had never once brought these precious indicators of his life downstairs to show them off to his friends or to his grandchildren, not even out of a sense of mild interest and amusement. He had less interest in revisiting his own past than I did.

Through the open door, I can hear the rhythms of his breathing. Under a mound of papers from the United Nations Association, I spot a large homemade notebook. The cover is made out of cardboard and blotchy green canvas and the spine has been roughly glued together and reinforced with two brass tacks.

Inside is a mass of dense typing on coarse green paper. The book, along with the accompanying UN documents, appear to be slowly gravitating towards the bin, my father no longer able to recall their purpose. I open the first page.

"The spirit of the opera," it begins, "moves me to commence to try to record in readable English the notes I wrote covering my experiences escaping from a prison camp in Italy during September and October 1943, just a year ago. I say the spirit of the opera because I start writing to the music of Leoncavallo's famous I Pagliacci even in name alone so very Italian and such a reminder of a lovely country so ill handled by Mussolini and his supporters."

It is the diary, I realise, of another prisoner. The ornate style suggests a very different character from the plainness of my father's writings. According to the cover page, his name is Tony MacDonnell, a name I immediately recognise. Colonel Tony MacDonnell was on the list of those who had been in Poppi and then travelled

"The Gloomy Dean", Richard Carver's fellow escaper

with Richard and the others to Fontanellato. He was known as the "Gloomy Dean" by the other prisoners, after Dean Inge, the Dean of St Pauls who was a figure in the 1930s fêted for his lugubrious outlook on life.

Just a year ago. He must have written his diary no later than 1944. I imagine him sitting by the window in some bachelor's apartment in Victoria with his gramophone playing his beloved Leoncavallo; the streets still buried in rubble from the Blitz.

A photograph of the "Dean" has survived in my father's papers. It shows him standing on the steps of a large country house, before the war. He has a moustache and is dressed in a tweed jacket, plus fours and a flat cap. A pipe sticks out of the corner of his mouth. He is striking something of a heroic pose, scanning the horizon with a shotgun at the ready, as if posed to bag a pheasant from the terrace of the house at any moment.

In the preface of the Journal I come across these words: "Richard Carver was my companion and guide. Without his leadership, I should have been the lost sheep in the wilderness. Richard did all the navigating, producing his homemade compass when we were in doubt, copying maps when we could not obtain them and, most of all, speaking to the Italians, never failing to make himself understood. He was marvellously patient with his silent companion and never showed the slightest sign of resentment when he had night after night to do all the begging."

The description jolts me. I have stumbled on an account of my father's experiences told not from his endlessly modest point of view but from the perspective of another man. In it is the unexpected image of my father as a leader.

9.

FOR THE INMATES of Fontanellato, the early evening of 8th September 1943 seemed no different from any other. The weather was hot and sultry, a low haze gathered on the horizon and the POWs sat in deckchairs in the shade of the watchtowers, watching a listless game of football.

On the other side of the wire, workers moved slowly through the vineyards with large wicker baskets slung from their shoulders, picking the first harvest of grapes. Rumours had circulated that morning that Monty was on the verge of landing on the Italian mainland from Sicily, but no one had taken much notice of them.

The six weeks since Mussolini's arrest had bought valuable time for General Kesselring, the German commander in Italy. He had managed to bring in ten divisions from Austria and Occupied France. His intention was to slow down the expected Allied advance up Italy long enough over the next three months to stop them from reaching Rome before Christmas. Once winter set in, any serious advance with armour would become impossible, giving the Germans a further breathing space to build more substantial defences.

News of the Eighth Army's successful advance had certainly improved morale in the camp, but Sicily was six hundred miles from Fontanellato. The Flying Fortresses were the only evidence of Allied troops they'd seen, whereas almost every day they could hear convoys of German troops passing southeast on the Via Emilia, the main Milan to Bologna road that ran half a mile to the south of the camp. Several units had stayed in the town on their way to the front.

Inside the old orphanage the heat was oppressive; men dozed on their beds, in Tommy's Bar they leaned out of the windows straining to catch a breeze. Following the fall of Mussolini, the guards had become more lenient, no longer firing back on sight at prisoners in the windows.

At about 7.30pm there was a disturbance down below in the courtyard. Suddenly, just like six weeks earlier, the guards began pouring out of their huts and shouting and dancing around each other.

"What's going on?" yelled the prisoners. "*Cosa succede?*"

"*Armistizio! Armistizio!*" the guards yelled up at the faces above them. A few moments later, Colonnello Vicedomini could be seen pushing his way through the crowd to his office in the orphanage. Prisoners ran out into the corridor and burst out into the exercise field to give the news. Italy had surrendered.

The order was given for all prisoners to assemble immediately in the main hall. Hugh Mainwaring, the man who had been captured with Richard in the desert, jumped onto a table and announced that an Armistice had been signed between the Allies and Italy, and that the SBO Colonel de Burgh was in discussions with the Colonnello about what to do.

"Remain calm and do not celebrate. It is not over yet," he said.

119

Into the vacuum poured rumours – the Germans were just outside the camp, there'd been a parachute landing by the Allies near Genoa, a sea landing at Rimini. Some claimed it would only be a matter of days before they were reunited with their regiments; others reminded them of the fighting ability of the German army.

People said that the guards were going to abandon the camp. Suddenly freedom seemed close at hand, but many privately dreaded the chaos and confusion of being "on the run"; instead of going home they were being tipped into a battleground. The camp, with all its curious habits and routines, now felt less of a prison and more like a sanctuary from the furious anarchy outside.

The Colonnello was pessimistic – if anything, the future was going to get worse, he told the SBO. His country now had two occupying armies, one from the north and one from the south, heading towards each other. Far from signalling peace, he believed that the Armistice was about to trigger a much more vicious war.

As far as he was concerned, Vicedomini was free to deal with his 600 British prisoners of war as he thought fit. The Italian War Office had ceased to exist. His government was in hiding. What he did with these POWs was a matter of his own conscience. The easiest option would have been to do nothing; the nearest German unit was rumoured to be only a few miles away. He could simply order his guards to lock the gates, return to the watch towers and wait for the Germans to arrive and take over, as many of the other camp commandants did. It took a brave and independent spirit to act otherwise. In the course of the next twelve hours it became clear where Vicedomini's true loyalties lay: he hated the presence of the Germans on Italian soil and wanted to see them beaten as much as the British did.

That evening, he informed SBO de Burgh that he had ordered his guards to prepare demolition explosives and dig trenches to defend the camp against a German attack. He then offered to let de Burgh send one POW out of the camp to reconnoitre a suitable

120

place to hide the prisoners in case the Germans arrived within the next few hours.

"I will provide my interpreter, Capitano Camino, to help him to communicate with the local population," he added.

De Burgh was grateful but sceptical; why would the locals suddenly help to keep the location of 600 escapees hidden? The few prisoners who had managed to escape had all been recaptured for the Italians were very good at distinguishing the fake from the genuine. Someone was bound to inform the Germans.

Nonetheless he told Hugh Mainwaring to go - it seemed fitting that someone who had been captured carrying out a reconnaissance should carry out another reconnaissance to orchestrate an escape. As the light started to fade, the two of them, Mainwaring and 'Cap' Camino, set off down the road past the convent on a pair of requisitioned bicycles.

De Burgh then approached Richard. As the most senior Royal Engineer officer in the camp, Richard was nominally 'in charge' of the 12 other Engineer officers. So far they had done nothing together except form a football team, but de Burgh was clearly determined to organise the camp on military lines, perhaps in preparation for a return to the battle.

"At first light you are to post your platoon of engineers at the gates. If the Italian guards vanish in the night, then you and your men are to take their place. You are to prevent any prisoner from leaving the camp by the main gate – by force if necessary. We must not allow a breakdown in order."

Other platoons were tasked with doing the same all along the wire. It was an invidious position to be in and one that Richard had never imagined might happen; to be taking over the guarding of a camp full of his colleagues inside enemy territory. It looked as if de Burgh was intending to implement the "stay put" order. The next day, Thursday 9th, he started his diary thus:

Truly a memorable day! Having got up at 0600 we found we were not needed as guards as the Italian sentries were still on duty. The others went back to bed but I stayed up and studied my bible in the growing light, wondering what the day would bring forth.

He could see several of the guards standing in newly dug slit trenches and an adjacent pig sty wearing glum expressions. They had no interest in fighting, especially not in a new war against the Germans. Then after breakfast came an order to prepare to move out at short notice. Everyone was told to take only one day's worth of rations.

As we only expected to be out a few hours, such was the unreality of the situation, we didn't take so much care in selecting articles to take with us as we might have done.

Richard's small band of engineers was tagged onto a company commanded by the Gloomy Dean – the man whose diary I was to find in my father's study. The Dean, however, like many other prisoners, seemed remarkably unaware of the precariousness of that day. In *his* diary he records going as usual to the bar for a pre-lunch aperitif: "The bar, as might be expected under the circumstances, was very well attended; spare tickets were difficult to obtain. It was when walking upstairs to return my glass to my room before going down to lunch that I met a lot of the other ranks all with their haversacks, running down; almost simultaneously the bugler sounded the alarm."

Two guards sent by the Vicedomini to find the exact location of the Germans had returned, saying that they'd seen a German convoy heading towards Fontanellato. Colonel de Burgh ordered everyone to line up by their companies on the exercise field. Richard rushed upstairs to try to recover the stash of Red Cross chocolate that he had been hiding just for such an eventuality, but he was pushed back by the crowds heading the other way.

"The Germans are moving fast," de Burgh announced as men

poured out of the building into the field. "They apparently know that the Orphanage at Fontanellato contains a large number British officer prisoners."

Shortly after midday, three Gs were blown by the camp bugler and Vicedomini ordered his guards to cut the barbed wire at the back of the exercise field. Company commanders reported their charges present and de Burgh announced the order of march; the Dean's company, with Richard's troop, was told to go last. As the Italians stood to one side in an impromptu guard of honour, the prisoners of PG49 marched out three at a time, saluting to the Senior British Officer as they passed as if they were on a parade ground.

It took some time for 600 men to pass through the small gap in the wire. At the back, Richard and his engineers waited anxiously for their turn. The moment seemed increasingly unreal. Any moment they expected to hear hoarse shouts of "Alt!" and the running of feet behind them in the orphanage, but nothing came. The Germans had stopped eight miles away to organise the evacuation of four labour camps – had they headed straight for the camp, they would have arrived with the escape still in progress.

As he inched towards the gap, Richard glanced back one last time at the playing field that had been his world; it was completely empty except for the four white geese. He remembered them as goslings scuttling in and out of the feet during the daily roll call and squawking for the safety of the stream during rugby games. Fattened by the guards all summer on a diet of lettuce and corn, the birds now huddled nervously together in the middle of the football pitch watching everyone leave. It was just after midday.

10.

To walk through the wire was like stepping through a looking-glass. It was a hot day; small puffs of cloud clotted the blue sky. After months of trying to escape with tunnels, in the end the men of PG49 had simply walked out. Suddenly they were in the world of farmers and peasant girls, of ox-drawn carts swaying under hillocks of hay and motorcars rattling past to market. The prospect of being killed by the Germans or the Italian fascists felt significantly greater than any danger they had faced as POWs. After months of captivity, most POWs had grown used to the routine and relative safety of prison life. To each other they had talked continuously about being home by Christmas and getting the chance to rejoin the fight against the Jerries, but in fact many were suffering from what was known in the German camps as *gefangenitis*, a torpor bordering on depression which came from being shut up for so long. In their walks in the countryside as POWs, the locals had been ordered to look the other way when they passed, but now, to the prisoners' relief, they were surrounded by smiling townspeople.

As they walked, the long line of soldiers kicked up a large dust

124

cloud; the front of the line was too far ahead for Richard to see. He got out his homemade compass, he could tell that they were being led northwest away from the town and out among the farms and fields. Farmers in their wide-brimmed straw hats stopped the harvesting to watch, and a few even cheered. Richard felt vulnerable not having any weapons – any moment he expected to see a line of grey German trucks on the horizon - ten well armed soldiers would be sufficient to arrest everyone.

They had been walking for about twenty minutes when there was a sudden noise of an aircraft. A German Junkers flashed low overhead. There was panic as hundreds of men attempted to lie down on the road at once. It took a long time – most prisoners were out of condition and Leon the Belgian cook, a rotund character whose girth seemed undiminished by captivity, fainted. A car appeared and out of it got a farmer with buckets of water which were passed down the line. The cook was bundled into the car and taken away.

A bit further along they stopped in the shade of a line of poplars. Richard could see a man in a pinstripe suit conferring with Cap in the shadows whilst all around prisoners sat smoking and listening to the unfamiliar sounds of the birds and the wind rustling the poplar leaves. No one spoke. De Burgh walked along the line explaining the plan; we're heading for a large wood nearby, he said, where we're to stay until the Germans have moved on.

"Nowhere is going to be big enough to hide us all," said one prisoner. "Someone is bound to betray us."

A couple of workers stood in the field on the other side of the road staring. They must have been a curious sight, these British men, a mixture of uniforms and old clothes, all still carrying the red flashes on their backs that signified Prisoner of War.

"Look at those Italians – any of them could tell the Germans where we are." Some of the officers began demanding that the group be broken up and for everyone to be allowed to go their own way. But de Burgh and Cap – the British and the Italian officer -

were in agreement: if we break into smaller groups we stand very little chance.

"We must hide until the hunt has died down; the Germans will never think of looking for us so close to the camp," said de Burgh. Richard knew it was an extraordinary gamble to try to hide everyone in one place but he also felt that this was probably the least worst option. He asked his friend Hugh Mainwaring if he'd found a good location when he went on the reconnaissance. "We have. It's well hidden from the air, but I can't tell until we get there whether we're all going to fit."

They moved off again. After another half an hour, Cap and Mainwaring led the straggling line of six hundred harried men off the road and down a track through an old vineyard. Between the vines, Richard could see the ground had been tilled. At the end of the field lay a small wood. Someone said the place was called Rovacchia. Richard estimated that they had walked no more than two miles from the camp. As he came out of the sunlight and adjusted his eyes to the gloom, he saw a steep bank below him covered in undergrowth leading down to a dry rocky riverbed. Hundreds of prisoners were already lying in the riverbed and all the way up either side squashed together, clutching their few possessions and panting in the heat.

"There's no space left; the wood is full!" said a voice.

The Dean was ordered to take his company of 100 men, including Richard's troop, back out to the field and hide among the vines. Richard's engineers grumbled. They felt very exposed; they were clearly visible from the sky. It was still several hours until darkness.

Richard lay with his face pressed down among the vine stalks and wondered what to advise the engineers under his command to do if the Germans arrived:

It was no good all bolting like rabbits or some would undoubtedly get shot, the only hope was to lie still, or possibly if they were round-

ing up people at the far end of the field to try and move off quietly along the vine row in the opposite direction.

A bottle of water was passed down, then came word that the Germans had reached the camp. Furious at finding it empty, the soldiers had begun looting the Red Cross supplies. One rumour claimed that they were getting drunk on the vermouth left behind in Tommy's Bar.

*

As the last prisoners had disappeared through the gap in the wire, Vicedomini had released his guards from their posts in the pig sty and the slit trenches and they had run to the guardroom, ripped off their uniforms and put on their civilian clothes; they had no interest in confronting the Germans and Vicedomini wasn't going to force them to fight over an empty camp whose only inmates were four white geese.

After they too had left, the Colonello returned to his office to put his papers in order. He was no longer answerable to any legal authority but he could not break the orderly habits of a professional soldier. He sat down at his desk and waited. He had carried out his duty and hoped that the idea of Italy would live on in its people even if the State no longer existed.

A little after 3pm the Germans pulled up in front of the Orphanage in a cloud of dust and truck fumes. There were about two hundred of them; they marched up the front steps and into the entrance hall. They scoured the rooms, noticing the signs of sudden departure; the beds unmade, many with the blankets missing, old tin cans and rations that no one wanted lying around. When they reached the exercise area and found the gap in the wire they turned on Vicedomini, screaming at him and kicking him. They told him he had betrayed the cause of fascism and national socialism and had insulted the name of the Führer.

A couple of the officers wanted to drag him to the exercise

yard and execute him at once. But a small crowd had gathered under the plane trees on the boulevard to watch what was going on. The Germans knew that they were not welcome as the new arrivals in Italy; a public execution might turn the local population into resistance. So they placed Vicedomini under arrest and dragged him down the steps of the *Orfanotrofio*.

Handcuffed and dishevelled, he was pushed into the back of a truck. It was the last time that the people of Fontanellato saw him. Vicedomini spent the rest of the war in a German labour camp. He managed to hold on until the Allied liberation. Well into his sixties and his health broken by the hard labour, he died shortly after returning to Italy, having lived just long enough to see a new Italian state emerge.

The German commander gave the order to get back into the trucks and start searching. It had only been a few hours, the prisoners could not have got very far. The patrols moved off in different directions, confident of soon seeing clumps of obvious-looking prisoners walking through the fields. It wasn't long before the rumble of the trucks reached Rovacchia.

Richard pressed his face harder into the soil. The sounds came closer. Several times the trucks and motorbikes passed right by the wood where hundreds of prisoners crouched in the shadows. The Germans must have wondered how so many could have vanished so completely.

As dusk fell, swarms of mosquitoes and midges began lifting off the bushes in the river bed, awakened by the cooling air. The sound of muffled curses and people trying to swat them away could be heard by Richard and the others lying in the fields. Had the Germans stopped for a moment on the road and cut their engines, they would have heard them too.

Darkness finally came around 8pm. Somehow they had done it. 600 men had slipped out of a Prisoner of War camp and hidden themselves right under the noses of the Germans. Or at least they had got through the first day, though there was still the possibility of betrayal. By now the entire village must know where they were.

As if to confirm their fears, groups of Italians began to appear at the edge of the wood. Then someone noticed Cap among them. The interpreter had gone out and sought food and water from neighbouring farms and he returned with several farmers laden with buckets of water, bread, grapes and hard dry chunks of parmesan. The Italians placed the food in the middle of the wood. Some of the prisoners held back at first, still struggling to grasp the idea that the battle lines had changed. They found it hard to trust Cap who had spent a year relaying the orders and punishments of the commandant and the guards. But gradually his transparently good nature won them over and to everyone's astonishment he revealed that he had an English wife and had even run a business in London before the war.

That night everyone had a different plan – to go north to the Swiss border, to strike out for the coast to greet the hoped for Allied landings, to hide in the farms nearby and wait for the Allies to get here, to head south on the long hike down the Apennines. Each idea could be argued with equal authority; the truth was that no one had a clue what was going on. The camp radio appeared to have vanished, left behind in the rush. They were more out of touch outside the camp than they had been inside it.

Already the evenings in the bar playing baccarat, the history classes, the amateur dramatics and the soccer tournaments seemed a distant memory. They faced a rough, uncertain future as the hunted. Hardly any of the prisoners could speak more than a few words of Italian. They were hiding in occupied territory and could be shot at any time as enemy combatants. Their chances of survival seemed slim - it would have been farcical if it wasn't so dangerous. Richard told his troop to ration themselves to a quarter of tin of bully beef and 2 biscuits a day.

At about 9pm the first group left, fortified by the food; and then more went, pushing past the others eager to get going. There was finally enough space in the wood for the Dean's company with my father's troop to be allowed off the fields and under cover. Many of them slept on the sloping ground exhausted by the day; others sat chatting, smoking and swatting the mosquitoes, adjusting themselves to the unaccustomed sounds of the night. They could hear the steady hum of German military traffic heading south on the Via Emilia. The occasional drone of transport planes filtered into the wood. Were they Allied or German?

The next morning Cap reappeared with several hundred loaves that the local baker had made overnight for the prisoners. With him came a farmer who had milked his entire herd to provide milk for them. He had civilian clothing too. Arguments quickly broke out as prisoners struggled to get rid of their battledress with the telltale red strip as fast as possible. Many were convinced that a single item of Italian peasants' clothes would make them invisible. Bad decisions were made. Thick warm battledress jackets were exchanged in haste for a camisole or a thin shirt. Others swapped their army boots for badly made shoes.

The Italians found it hard not to laugh at the sight of these pale, earnest British officers squeezing themselves into ill fitting *contadini* trousers. One officer, Douglas Flowerdew, decided the safest way of avoiding attention was to dress as a woman. The farmers' wives fitted him out with a blue stockinette dress, a blue kerchief padded with maize hair on his head and high heels. Everyone laughed at the sight, but he managed to get all the way back to England where he became a vicar in Sussex after the war.

Another group of locals arrived with Red Cross parcels from the camp. The temptation to have taken this food home must have been considerable, but instead they handed them to the POWs. They said there was little sign today of the Germans at the camp. Buoyed by this news the prisoners became more confident. They began to walk around more freely; a few of the prisoners lucky enough to have secured a flagon of wine even held a picnic among the vines.

One of the local farmers invited prisoners to stay in his barn and took the first 14 who raised their hands. By being in the barn rather than the house, he could claim that they had hidden in there without him realising. He promised to bring them food and water when he could. His example was followed by others and through-out the night, small groups were led away by local farmers.

Late that afternoon, de Burgh called his company command-ers together for the final time. From tonight onwards, he said, each company was on its own. Each commander was told to decide whether to break up into smaller groups, to stay, or to move off. When the Dean returned with the news, Richard called a vote among his 12 men on what they wanted to do: about one third wanted to head north to the Swiss border, others voted to try to reach the Gulf of Genoa, believing that the Allies might land raid-ing parties in the area.

During that day as he sat in the wood, Richard had formed his own plan: he had decided he was going to try to walk south down the Apennines to find his stepfather. It was the furthest of all the options and much depended on how quickly the Eighth Army was able to battle its way north – at that moment Monty had only a toehold on the Italian mainland five hundred miles to the south - but Richard was sceptical of talk about landing parties and rescu-ers coming from the sea and he didn't like the idea of sitting still, hiding in someone's barn, as many were choosing to do, to wait for the Allies to get to them.

To his surprise, once he was out of the camp, he found that he wanted to keep moving. He had enjoyed the life of Fontanel-lato and had felt the occasional twinge of guilt for not having tried more actively to escape. Perhaps there was a desire to show Monty what he was capable of, though he wouldn't have acknowl-edged it.

He could hardly conceive how many obstacles lay ahead. He was heading into the eye of the battle. To reach Monty meant hav-ing to dodge through the German forces, by approaching them from the rear and breaking out across the front line. If he wasn't killed by the Germans he stood a good chance of being killed by artillery or bombing by his own forces. Even now, the Germans were building a series of heavily defended lines stretching across the country from Rome to the Adriatic coast. Five of his men decided to join him on the route south:

I took a vote of the remainder of my platoon (Hargreaves, Hartley, Bligh, Lyndon and Clyma) and they were in favour of making a bid for it.

Just then the Dean approached Richard to ask if he could join them. He explained that all bar five of his company had formed their own groups. Just he and his small headquarters staff remained. Richard was reluctant: six people was already a lot, 12 would be much harder to hide. But he felt he could not say no, after all the Dean was a colonel and Richard was only a captain. Richard assumed that the Dean would take over command, but the Dean showed no sign of wanting the responsibility and it was tacitly agreed that Richard would lead, despite being the junior of the two. He had the compass, the map and a rudimentary grasp of Italian. He had diligently attended a few classes in camp and knew enough words to make himself understood.

Towards dusk, reports started to trickle back from POWs who'd left the night before that there were large numbers of German troops guarding the Via Emilia and the Bologna-Milan railway which ran side by side only three miles away. One party was even rumoured to have turned back. This was something of a blow. Richard knew that the railway and the road lay directly in their path; if they wanted to head south they had no choice but to cross them both.

11.

IT WAS A CLEAR night with a full moon. They walked for six miles, guided by the sound of goods trains shunting through the darkness. Richard had decided to try and find a crossing point some distance away from the place where the others had attempted it. As they drew near, he sent a scout ahead to try to find out where the German guards were, but he returned having failed to get close enough to see. Hargreaves was then sent to try; after twenty minutes, a dog began barking furiously at a nearby farm. Worried that Hargreaves might have been captured, Richard told everyone to pull back. He then sent out a third scout who by luck managed to find Hargreaves in the dark. Hargreaves whispered that there was a German sentry less than 20 yards ahead. Unused to being on the run, it took the two of them a long time to crawl clumsily away.

Just before dawn, the twelve POWs managed to cross the road and the railway line. Exhausted by their efforts, they collapsed into a wood beside a small river near the village of Santa Margherita. They had travelled all of seven miles from the wood at Rovacchia. Like all the others they had brought minimal amounts of food with them from the camp. As they sat in the wood it was obvious that they would never survive unless they were helped by the local Italians. The first encounters with the locals in Rovacchia had been positive, but how could they tell who were pro-Allies and who were Fascists?

They were desperate for water, but no one volunteered for the job of being the first to find out. Richard was hardly keen but he approached the nearest farmhouse and knocked on the door. *"Avete un po' di acqua?"* he asked hesitantly, when a stout-looking woman opened the door.

Without saying a word, she indicated with her head where the pump stood in the corner of the farmyard.

"Grazie."

Richard went back to the others and one by one the twelve of them went up to the farm to have a drink and wash under the pump, watched through the net curtains by the family. They waited until dark before leaving. Away from the road and the railway line there was little evidence of Germans so Richard insisted that his group march in formation to maintain as much speed as possible. Passing through a small hamlet a group of Italians who had been sitting in the road ran away when they saw them approach, thinking they were Germans. Richard wrote in his diary:

> *It was only with great difficulty that I managed to coax them out.*
> *Then when they realised we were English they couldn't do enough*
> *for us and wine was produced though it was near midnight. Halted*
> *at 0130 in a pretty little valley.*

The next day, they decided to start walking in the late afternoon. Despite the nervousness of the locals the previous night, there was little sign of enemy presence away from the main roads. Marching briskly along the lanes, they grabbed bunches of grapes off the vines as they passed. They began to relax, savouring the joy of being on an open road and no longer in captivity. The warm September sun browned their arms and they pointed out to each other the distant medieval castles and the teams working in the fields who waved occasionally as they passed. It almost felt as if they were on a walking holiday.

About nine o'clock that evening, as they were passing a house, someone yelled out a greeting in English. They stopped and found that the owner of the house was an American woman. She advised them to head towards a small village called Contile which she said was friendly. It sat atop a precipitous hill and it was nearly midnight when they entered the cobbled streets which wrapped themselves around the church in the centre like the tail of a snake. Richard saw a light on in a workshop and knocked on the door. Inside, several men were trying to mend a piece of machinery. Richard asked if there was a barn they could spend the night in. As one of the workers led them out to his farm, most of the village trailed after them in the warm darkness, fascinated by the sight of twelve Englishmen on the run.

They sank into the hay, relieved to be no longer be lying on the stony ground. The next morning, being a Sunday, the Dean, who was a catholic, decided it was safe enough to attend mass in the village church. It was in Latin which the Dean understood better than Italian. Afterwards outside the church, an elderly widow approached him outside the church, clutching a postcard from her son sent from England. The Dean gathered that he was in a POW camp outside London. She had heard from him only once, she said.

She insisted that the whole group go to her tiny cottage to view her son's picture.

"How is he being cared for? The postcard says nothing," she said, her voice full of the pain of separation.

"He will be properly treated," Richard assured her.

They told the villagers that they were going to lie up for the day in a nearby beech wood; by the time they got there, a number of villagers had already arrived with pots and pans and had begun to build a fire for them. Children came to gaze at the unusual

135

visitors bringing with them gifts of bread, fatty bacon and eggs from their parents. One man brought his axe and showed them how to chop up wood into small staves to make a proper outdoor stove for cooking.

Spent the day in a field outside the village where we 'received' visitors. Listened to the wireless which was depressing. No mention of any landings further north than Salerno and things don't seem to be going too well there. We must split up tomorrow.

They wondered where all the other prisoners were and whether any of them had been captured. They were surprised not to have come across anyone else; it was as if the countryside had swallowed them up. They leant back against the trees and discussed what to do, watched always by an outer ring of curious onlookers. Everyone agreed that the further south they travelled the more concentrated the German forces would become. It was clear that twelve was too big a number for a group in hiding, and it was decided to split up into twos and threes.

Richard offered to go with the Dean. He could tell that no one else was keen to travel with him, they were worried that his age would slow them down. Moreover, the temptation for someone to betray them was much greater because the reward for handing in a senior British officer like a colonel was considerable, and the punishment for sheltering one grievous.

The next morning, they pooled the money that they had each been given before leaving camp and then divided it equally between everyone. It came to 147 lire each. Someone divided up what was left of the Red Cross food which worked out to one tin of meat and one packet of biscuits each. They made copies of each other's maps and those who could not speak Italian hurriedly wrote out lists of useful Italian words.

At two pm, after one last meal together, Richard and the Dean said goodbye to the others and moved out. In the next village they came to, they exchanged their British uniforms for civilian clothes. For some reason the only clothes that were on offer were two thin blue suits; Richard's was too short in the leg and the Dean's didn't button up at the front, but they both held onto their army boots and Richard kept his thick battledress jacket. The Dean acquired an Italian army haversack and Richard made a backpack from an old grain sack.

They made an odd pair; the Dean twenty years older than Richard, puffing up the hills with his walking stick, always hoping that around the next corner would be a little farmhouse where he could sit beside the fire in the farmer's kitchen and have a cigarette and always hoping that a cup of wine, some bread and cheese and possibly a bowl of pasta might come his way. Richard, earnest and energetic, was constantly checking their route, worrying about the progress of the war and trying to ferret information out of the farmers' families about the dangers ahead. Their accounts of their journey together are markedly different in style: Richard's is low key, succinct and practical, clocking each passing day with a minimum of flourish. The Dean's, written shortly after he returned home but based on the notes he kept on the run, is full of detail about the places that they travelled through, and particularly the food they ate and the places in which they slept. For him, the progress of the war itself was no more than a background nuisance, like inclement weather on a camping holiday.

Richard asked the Dean to tell everyone they met that he was a captain not a colonel to attract less attention. The Dean, who wore his colonelcy lightly, was happy to oblige. Their differences in age and temperament were what made the relationship work. As Richard shrewdly noted, he might well have quarrelled with a man of his own age, "whereas the Dean practically always agreed to what I proposed."

In those opening days when the weather was still warm and there was little sign of danger, my father's diary conveys the impression of a young man delighted to be free, someone open to adventure. The two of them carried nothing in their backpacks, except a few articles of clothing, chunks of bread. the occasional bunch of grapes, or dried figs or hard-boiled egg if they were fortunate enough to be given one. My father also carried a bible sent to him in camp by Aunt Bulley. They relied from one day to the next on the hospitality of others.

Richard clearly enjoyed the process of talking with the locals and choosing the route. They soon gave up trying to work out who the fascists were – it seemed like no one was nostalgic for Mussolini, or if they were, they kept it well hidden. Starved of company and distractions in the countryside, people would walk alongside the two British men every time they entered a village, peppering them with questions.

"Where is your family and your *casa?*"

"How long will it take to walk to *Inghilterra?*"

"*Poveri ragazzi!*"

Then would come the invitation to have a drink which the Dean was always quick to accept. Extra chairs would be brought and a circle would form around them in the street while the shy stood and stared. The men who had fought alongside the British in the First World War and those who had worked in America were the most willing to talk. The villages of central Italy were well used to the presence of conquering armies. The *contadini* – the Italian peasant farmers – had often lived under the rule of distant powers. They had a fierce independence and a lively sympathy for anyone who bucked the system; had it been the Allies who were winning, they may well have helped German prisoners to flee in the opposite direction.

*

On 20th September, twelve days after they had left Fontanellato, Richard and the Dean entered a small village near Busana. At first everything seemed normal. The locals said they had seen large numbers of Germans passing through the area heading south but none had stayed. They were invited to an inn where they were offered some eggs. They asked if they could be boiled and while they waited, two glasses of Marsala appeared. As they sat drinking in the tiny front room, the doorway crowded as usual with curious faces staring in as if they were zoo animals, an argument began between some communists and monarchists. The communists said that the British and Americans were only playing at war and claimed that the only true fighters were the Russians. Suddenly a woman broke through the two camps yelling, "*Tedeschi! Tedeschi!*"

There was panic as the inn emptied into the street while two German soldiers tried to force their way through. Richard and the Dean grabbed their sacks and raced out the back door of the pub, through a garden and over a low fence. The Dean, slower and older, tried to jump the fence and failed. One of the Germans emerged from the inn and yelled at him to stop. But he managed to get up and half fall, half clamber over the rickety wooden structure to run down the slope after Richard. For several hours they lay on an island in a dry riverbed listening for sounds of pursuit but none came. It was their first brush with the Germans – a sign that life was going to become more challenging.

After that, they decided to stay on the high ground following the backbone of the Apennines which ran down Italy, where there were fewer roads and centres of population and which the Germans had little interest in occupying. Food in the hillside farms was still fairly plentiful. At every stop they would be given bread and cheese and often polenta, which the Dean ate only with the greatest reluctance. Eggs and tomatoes were more precious, and pasta, which had to be made by hand. If they were hungry as they walked, they would pull blackberries off the bushes and the roads were lined with vineyards full of ripe grapes.

Every night they slept in barns rather than the open - and occasionally when luck was on their side the farmer invited them into his house if he felt sure that there were no Germans nearby. The children would usually be turfed out of their beds to make way for the guests and in the morning there would be a cup of coffee and a piece of fresh bread. Usually they would be expected to leave at the same time as the farmer went out to work in the fields; Richard learnt not to ask to stay more than one night.

During the final week of September, the weather started to deteriorate. The long bucolic summer evenings were replaced by several days of slanting rain. Their thin Italian cotton suits were quickly soaked through. They crossed the main Bologna-Pistoia road narrowly missing a convoy of German trucks that sped past full of soldiers. There were lots of rumours that the Allies had landed nearby on the coast at Livorno, but when Richard finally managed to listen to the BBC in a house, the news was disappointing. On the east coast, Monty had moved quickly up as far as Bari – the port where Richard had been interned nearly a year earlier – but was now encountering strong resistance while the Americans were still trying to fight their way out of Naples after landing in Salerno.

On Friday 1st October, hidden in the middle of a huge beech wood, the trees still thick and green, they came across the Eremo dei Frati Bianchi, the Hermitage of the White Friars, which had been built by the followers of St Francis in the 13th century. They could see the huts of the hermits on the slopes behind the main building as they approached.

Richard rang the bell, while the Dean waited around the corner in case of an unfriendly reception. The door was opened by a well fed monk who laughed at their caution and waved at the Dean to come out of the shadows.

"We have another British officer resting here who is sick," said the monk.

"Can we see him?" asked Richard.

They were shown into a monk's cell where they found an Englishman dressed in pyjamas and lying in clean sheets looking perfectly healthy.

"Good afternoon. I'm the 6th Earl of Ranfurly."

The Dean recorded the moment in his diary:

We saw Lord R. in almost forgotten luxury, sitting up in bed with the remains of a very good lunch of mutton and wine on a tray by his side, and although one could hardly complain of the cold, a nice fire in the grate completed the perfect sick room. Lord R. looked far from death sitting up smoking a cigarette. He told us he had come in the previous day suffering from a slight cold.

The Earl explained that he was General Neame's ADC and that he had escaped from a POW camp near Florence. Hoping for the same kind of service as the Earl, Richard and the Dean were disappointed to be shown into a cold cell with two mattresses on the floor and no fireplace. Other POWs had clearly been before them, for the floor was littered with old tins and newspaper. "I didn't realise that Franciscans were so attuned to the requirements of the British aristocracy," the Dean muttered sourly.

Two days later they found themselves looking down on a familiar sight – the small neat walls of Poppi and the Villa Ascensione standing on the next door hill. "It was a rather strange feeling to look down on it from the outside, when we had so often looked up from the inside." They had been on the run for 25 days and in that time they estimated they had walked at least 200 miles, allowing for diversions and wrong turns – 8 miles a day.

"Doesn't sound very much," murmured the Dean as they sat in the woods looking down on the little railway line that had delivered them to the gates of Poppi from Bari.

"*Piano, piano ma sicuro, sicuro* – better to go slowly but safely," said Richard. "I don't want to get recaptured."

Apart from the Earl, they had not encountered any other POWs. It was as if they were travelling in some bubble separated in time and distance from the carnage that they knew was happening across the continent of Europe. They listened to the bells of La Verna calling the faithful to prayer – the Tuscan countryside, flooded with evening light, could not have looked less like a battle-field. "This can't last," said Richard.

*

As October wore on, the weather grew colder and the country-side became steeper and wilder. The wind turned into a raw angry presence that harassed and harried them everywhere they went. Some days they walked for several hours through rainstorms with-out seeing a building or person; when they reached a cottage they would shelter in a barn hoping that the farmer would take pity on them and let them in to the kitchen to dry out.

11th day	19th Sep 43	Sunday	A lovely day. Hos·
12th day	20th Sep 43	Monday	A close shave.
13th day	21st Sep 43	Tuesday	Trousers patched.
14th day	22nd Sep 43	Wednesday	Blackberry stew -
15th day	23rd Sep 43	Thursday	Double bed - lunc
16th day	24th Sep 43	Friday	Nasty crossing -
17th day	25th Sep 43	Saturday	Rest - good lunch
18th day	26th Sep 43	Sunday	Wind - Rats (long
19th day	27th Sep 43	Monday	Rain - Mill - wet
20th day	28th Sep 43	Tuesday	Good breakfast -
21st day	29th Sep 43	Wednesday	Wet again - early
22nd day	30th Sep 43	Thursday	Long walk - good
23rd day	1st Oct 43	Friday	With good friends
24th day	2nd Oct 43	Saturday	Failed to make it
25th day	3rd Oct 43	Sunday	Rest - disappoint
26th day	4th Oct 43	Monday	Lovely day - barn
27th day	5th Oct 43	Tuesday	Mass & b/fst - ha
28th day	6th Oct 43	Wednesday	3 B/fst - good b:
29th day	7th Oct 43	Thursday	Passed by lorry -
30th day	8th Oct 43	Friday	Gd B/fst -stayed
31st day	9th Oct 43	Saturday	Only 2 hrs rest.
32nd day	10th Oct 43	Sunday	Left after soup,
33rd day	11th Oct 43	Monday	Fm at top of hil
34th day	12th Oct 43	Tuesday	Early lunch(Tob)
35th day	13th Oct 43	Wednesday	B/F.Washed cloth
36th day	14th Oct 43	Thursday	High climb - fog
37th day	15th Oct 43	Friday	Snack B/F-refill
38th day	16th Oct 43	Saturday	Over mountains,r
			Americans at
39th day	17th Oct 43	Sunday	Wet climb,lunch

Transcript of daily entries from "The Dean's" diary

At every opportunity Richard would ask if there was a radio and then sit patiently turning the dial through the squelches and the static for any fragment of English voices or the reassuring notes of the BBC's Lilliburlero theme tune while the Dean puffed his pipe by the fire, happily oblivious to the fact that he was sitting in the farmer's favourite chair. The news of the war was not getting any better. Between the Germans and the Eighth Army somewhere to the south lay the Gran Sasso, the highest peak of the Apennines. Richard had hoped that Monty and Allies would reach the Gran Sasso before winter set in avoiding the need for them to cross it but now that seemed impossible. Even in summer the mountain was a daunting obstacle to cross but it was impossible to navigate in winter. There seemed little choice but to press on.

Over the next few days, they noticed that food was becoming steadily scarcer and the farms increasingly poor. They left behind the flat valleys littered with medieval towns and villages and found themselves walking higher into the mountains. No longer was the countryside filled with vines and fruit; there were long fingers of sheep meadowland sliced on either side by dark wooded ravines. They crossed a fast mountain stream where they saw the head of a sheep wedged in the rocks and the body forty feet below, torn apart by the force of the water.

In vast chestnut forests they swept up handfuls of nuts and mushrooms into their bags and began lighting fires in the day to keep warm, roasting their chestnuts. It was now hours between farms. And they had walked off the maps they had carried since camp – Richard felt curiously blind as if they were wandering in a limbo. From now on, they had to rely on Richard's compass for direction. It was a fragile instrument that had to be flattered rather than bullied into service.

When they did encounter farms, the inhabitants were usually quietly hospitable, and the Dean rarely missed an opportunity to enthuse about a good meal: "11th October. 33rd day on the run. We came to a farm perched on the end of a promontory. It was a communal farm with several families occupying one building, somewhere near Bivio. They used one kitchen and all fed together. The place was practically in darkness, except for what light the burning twigs gave off, supplemented later by an oil boat lamp and a very temperamental acetylene lamp which judging by the noises it made might have exploded any minute. One by one the party began to assemble, the men folk as usual occupying the available chairs near the fire.

"The cauldron for so large a party, for I think we must have been in the region of twenty, was of appropriate size. The water was boiling in the massive vessel hanging over the fierce fire by the heavy chain, supported somewhere up the chimney. A quantity of dried beans and peas mixed with barley was poured in, well stirred and allowed to boil. The cauldron was removed and placed on the table. Our plates were first filled to the brim and passed to us, the other men were then given helpings, the women recovering a lesser portion. Some of the women, unable to obtain a place at the table, ate their suppers with their children standing in the background."

Their paths continued upwards for another three days.

"Wind has dropped a bit but still pretty cold," Richard wrote, "probably because we are so high. Climbed over a mountain which cannot have been less than 7,000 feet and got lost on the top of a pass in the cloud."

As they were resting near the summit a mist swept in, blotting out all visibility. They stood up and walked on what they thought was the right path but after ten minutes, the Dean claimed he'd seen the same rock twice. From his pocket, Richard pulled out the little tin and extracted his compass; sure enough it showed them they were heading back the way they had come.

Up ahead they could see the peak of the Gran Sasso already covered in a fresh coating of powder. They fingered their thin cotton suits nervously; the plan for going south depended on the Allies being able to fight their way north in time. In their naivety they had left Fontanellato camp with hardly any supplies, and now, more

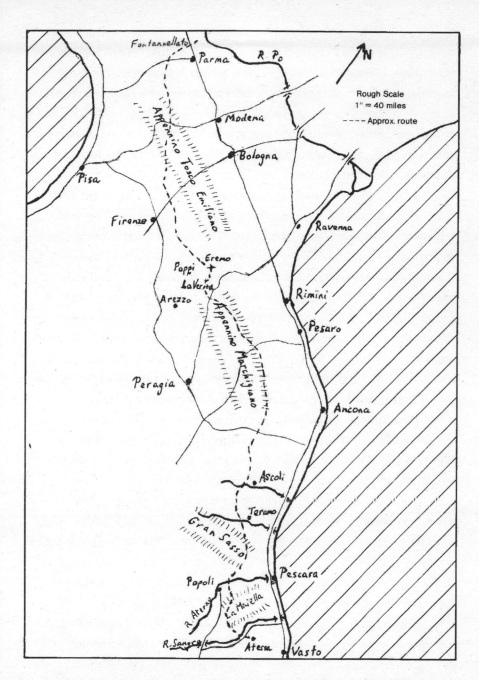

The map of his escape route, from Richard's wartime diary

than a month later, they still had far to go.

At high altitude, these farms barely had enough to feed themselves and what little extra they had they were husbanding for the cold nights that lay ahead. The peasants were also becoming increasingly nervous about being caught. Although Richard and the Dean could not have imagined it on their long isolated walks through the woods, from all over Italy, thousands of German and Allied soldiers were closing in on a frontline that ran roughly from Monte Cassino in the west across the country to the Adriatic coast. Their paths were about to converge with hundreds of escaped prisoners who were also heading to the front in the hoping of reaching the Allied side.

One of them was Carol Mather, Richard's old childhood friend who he had encountered in PG49. He had walked out of Fontanellato with all the others but as soon as the POWs had arrived at the ditch, he and another prisoner had slipped away on their own without waiting for any orders. They'd walked south as fast as possible and had managed to get through the mountains of the Abruzzo while the weather was still warm and there were still shepherds on the high pastures to give them food. They slipped through the German lines before they were fully established and reached Monty's Headquarters by the Biferno River on 15th October 1943. The whole trip had taken six weeks.

On the 19th October Monty wrote to the Reynoldses, David's guardians: "Carol Mather has escaped from his POW camp in Italy, came in through my front, and is now safe and well at my Army H.Q. Will you telephone the Mathers and let her know; I think it is Putney 4259. I have written to Louis Mather but she may get your message first if he is away. Dick escaped at the same time, but they got separated and Carol does not know where he is. I have great hopes he may appear soon. There are of course a great many POW wandering about Italy in peasants' clothes, and the Germans are trying hard to collect them in and have offered very large rewards to the Italians to give them away.

"You should stop sending parcels to Dick until we know more as to his whereabouts."

In fact, Richard and the Dean were a hundred miles away but the gap was closing all the time, as they kept moving south and Monty continued his advance north. Somewhere below Paranesi, they came across an ominous sign: an Italian artillery gun lying beside the road, mangled and disfigured. The locals told them that instead of surrendering their position like their colleagues, a few Italian soldiers had turned the gun on the Germans and opened fire. For one brave hour they became partisans, until the Germans stormed their position and blew up the gun.

Waiting in a ravine about to cross the Teramo-L'Aquila road, the sound of a car made them hesitate. Round the corner came two German motorbikes followed by a staff car with a general and his staff officer in the back. Richard and the Dean could see the medals glinting on their coats. Behind them came a truck with a machine gun mounted in the back and the crew standing beside it ready to open fire.

The next morning, they were chased out of a barn before dawn by the owner who claimed that a German convoy was approaching. The farmer said that German patrols had recently raided the village across the river. Richard and the Dean fled up the side of a hill and eventually arrived at a small farmhouse belonging to an elderly shepherd and his wife. All this couple could offer Richard and the Dean to eat were chestnuts and lard. She was about to wrap them in an official-looking piece of paper when Richard noticed the signature of Kesselring on the paper. "What is this?" he asked. "*Cos'è questo?*"

"It's a notice from the Germans," said the shepherd's wife. "We were ordered to pin it up in the village last week."

The poster described a long list of forbidden activities and offences. The punishment for assisting British or American prisoners was death by firing squad and the burning of any farm that had harboured them. As they read it out, the shepherd's wife laughed and finished rolling up their small gift. Richard was stunned by the unflinching bravery of these people. After they had eaten the lard and chestnuts, Richard and the Dean used the poster as toilet paper.

12.

EACH MORNING, RICHARD noticed that the saucer of snow lying in one of the shoulders of the Gran Sasso had grown in the night. The cold and malnourishment began to wear away at their reserves of energy; they felt tired as soon as they started in the mornings.

When Richard knocked on doors to ask for food and shelter, he encountered more and more excuses, often accompanied by a glitter of fear in the faces of those who stared back at him – we have already eaten, a German patrol came past this morning, we looked after a prisoner the night before... The days of leisurely walks and replete suppers of pasta and a smoke afterwards began to fade as they found themselves scavenging in the fields for the occasional potato that had been missed by the peasants.

Once a shepherd and his child offered to share their lunch with the Dean after they spotted him looking hungrily at their picnic; the gesture shamed him into declining.

On Friday October 22nd, as they were clambering across a stream early one morning, a farmer in a nearby field spotted them and ran after them. "Some American parachutists are hiding at a nearby farm," he said. When Richard arrived at the farm, he was surprised to find the parachutists still in bed. They said they were there to help organise POWs in preparation for evacuation. But they seemed listless and depressed.

"The Germans are massing in strength on the Pescara river," they explained. "The Italians around here all tell you it's now impossible to get through to the Allied lines this winter."

General Kesselring's defensive lines across Italy were starting to pay off. The first line which followed the Volturno river had been hastily assembled in the summer soon after Mussolini's arrest; it had been intended only to delay the Allies long enough for the Germans to be able to build bigger defences further north. Next came the Barbara Line on the Trigno River which ran into the sea just north of Termoli, then the Gustav Line on the Sangro River thirty miles north and finally the Caesar Line on the Pescara River another thirty miles north again. Each one, built by the Organisation Todt, the engineering company of the Nazis, using thousands of conscripted Italian soldiers, consisted of more and more elaborate artillery positions and fortifications. The last two, Caesar and Gustav, were known collectively as the Winter Line.

"Kesselring's plan is to hold us south of Rome long enough for winter to set in," said the parachutists. "Once the snows come, it'll be very hard for any Allied tanks to move. That will give him four months to bring in enough reinforcements to defend the Italian capital." They advised Richard and the Dean to find a warm farm and stay put until spring, which is what they themselves were apparently doing. Large numbers of POWs were gathering behind the lines, unable to move through. Several of the farms Richard and the Dean tried were already full, and they were told that the Germans, unhappy about the presence of British soldiers behind their positions, were conducting house to house raids. On the 21st October, Richard and the Dean debated their situation:

The question is whether to go on, and risk the difficulties of food

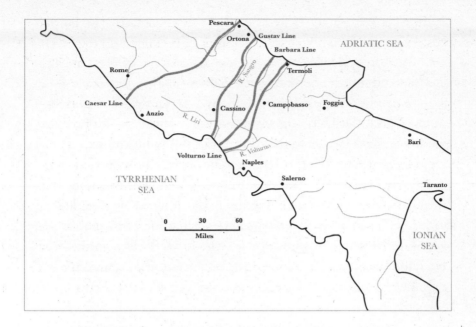

General Kesselring's defensive lines across Italy

*shortages and the increasing dangers of capture or stay put and hope
our forces will arrive soon. After a short mental prayer for guidance
I decided quite definitely in my own mind that the right thing was to
go on, and the Dean agreed.*

They may have been heading straight towards the enemy but
staying put seemed equally risky if not more so; sooner or later,
someone would tip off the Germans. So long as they were moving
they were still free.

The next morning, as Richard and the Dean were walking
down through a field of stubble near the village of Celiera, they
saw a figure striding confidently up towards them. As he came
closer, Richard thought he looked familiar. He realised that it was
another POW, whom Richard had trained with at the start of his
military career. His name was Major Gordon – for some reason
neither Richard nor the Dean recorded his first name in their

diaries – a big, ginger-haired Scottish officer from the Royal Signals Regiment.

Gordon told them that he had escaped from PG21, the camp in Chieti where the Senior British Officer had put guards on the gate to prevent anyone leaving. For two days, he had hidden in a tunnel whilst the Germans moved around above his head. Eventually the sounds had vanished and he had found himself alone, crept over the wall and disappeared into the hills. At that stage, he was less than a hundred miles from the Allied lines and there were far fewer Germans in the area. But for reasons best known to himself, instead of heading south, he had decided to stay and appointed himself as protector for the other POWs in the area. He had mastered only a few words of Italian which he spoke in a broad Glaswegian accent. The major agreed that the Pescara river was heavily guarded.

"They've got sentries all along the north bank," he said. "The best way out is by sea."

He said he had managed to make contact with the Eighth Army by sending a message on a fishing boat down the coast to the port of Termoli which had recently fallen to the Allies. This piece of news cheered Richard considerably. Termoli was less than eighty miles away. The Allies had replied with a message that they would be willing to evacuate some of the POWs. When Gordon heard this, he had ordered one of the officers, a Captain 'Badger' Light, to go down to the coast to organise the evacuation while he rounded up groups of prisoners. Badger Light had not yet returned, but Richard and the Dean agreed to join in the evacuation plan; it seemed like one that might work. Certainly, the prospect of a short if hazardous boat ride was more appealing than a long uncertain hike over the mountains.

Two days passed. There was still no sign of Captain Light and Richard began to get anxious. As a backup, he suggested that he and Gordon go down to reconnoitre the Pescara river to see if the reports of large numbers of German troops were true. They set off after dark and walked through the night. It had been agreed that Richard would take the western end of the river; Frank, an amiable Serb officer, the middle; and Gordon the east. Just before dawn, Richard could see in the distance flares being dropped by Allied planes on the coast – it was the first sighting he'd had of his own troops since leaving Fontanellato nearly two months before. He stood in the middle of a field gazing at the silent pyrotechnics on the horizon.

As it was getting light, he met a shepherd boy who guided him down to a spot close to the river where they were able to watch a road bridge; traffic seemed to be light and there were few guards. He was moving nearer to the road when a German patrol came around the corner. Richard squatted quickly down near the verge pretending to be inspecting the crops in the field as it passed a few yards away. He then withdrew to a barn and waited for night to arrive.

That evening he walked east until he came to a dam on the river where he found a house. An elderly woman let him stay in the attic and in the early hours her husband came home drunk, complaining loudly that the Germans had stolen his umbrella. The following night, Richard returned to Carpineto where the Dean was staying with the local schoolmaster. The others were already there. Frank the Serb described how he had persuaded an old woman to lead him across a bridge pretending to be her son. They had walked right passed the German sentries without being challenged, had taken a look around and walked back. Gordon said that he found no place in his area where they could cross.

As they were comparing notes in the schoolmaster's kitchen, there was a knock at the door and in walked 'Badger' Light, accompanied by two French commandos – "terrible-looking villians armed with sten guns" was the Dean's description. When the commandos took off their tunics they revealed bandoleers of ammunition across their chests. The schoolmaster stepped back with a panic-stricken look on his face; it was one thing to be caught harbouring unarmed escapers, but these were combat soldiers. Light dumped a stock of maps and English cigarettes onto the farmhouse table, and announced that everything was in place. He described how he had smuggled himself down to Termoli on a fishing boat and had spent 24 hours there arranging the rescue operation.

The French commandos did not offer any explanation as to why they were there. But Light explained that the French commandos had been provided to help guide the prisoners to the assembly area and to protect them in case they were attacked.

"I have identified an assembly area near Silvi Marina," said Light. "For two nights running a motor torpedo boat will come into one of the bays. They will flash a code with a torch. Once the POWs have responded with the right message, the boat will drop anchor and the party will wade out to it."

Gordon decided to send groups of 20 prisoners at a time down to the assembly point. Sitting in the kitchen smoking the English cigarettes, with the French commandos cleaning their weapons silently in the corner, the plan looked good. "We were all delighted at the idea," Richard commented, "and thought it sounded as if it would be a really good show this time."

It was agreed that the Dean should be on the first boat out; he would go at once to the coast with Badger Light and the French, while Richard and Gordon went round the farms briefing the other POWs. It was Saturday October 30th 1943. The Dean handed over his watch and beloved pipe to Richard. They had travelled well over 400 miles in each other's company, sharing beds at night and helping each other through each day. They shook hands and congratulated each other on getting this far. The Dean promised to send a note to Monty telling him that Richard was alive as soon as he reached Allied lines.

"I'll be home by morning!" he declared.

The first twelve prisoners were brought to the farmhouse. The schoolmaster generously cooked them a special meal of spaghetti followed by roast chicken, relieved no doubt to see them leave. At

2pm they set off. The French commandos, brushing aside concerns about Germans, marched the group straight down the road in full daylight. Several of the prisoners were still dressed in British uniforms.

"The contrast between the care and caution which Richard and I always observed to this free and easy crowd was remarkable," wrote the Dean.

He proposed that they split into two groups to reduce the chances of being killed in the event of an attack. This was agreed but within half an hour the groups had remerged since the one at the back, anxious not to lose the way, kept running into the one at the front. When they halted outside a farm to have a smoke, a German tank came round the corner and they ducked inside a barn.

An Italian ran out in to the road and warned them that there were Germans everywhere up ahead and told them to return to the hills but the French continued, full of *sang froid*.

A short distance further on, another Italian came alongside them on a bicycle and asked if they were heading to Silvi. They pretended never to have heard of the place. The Italian shrugged.

"Oh, I thought you might like to know that a British boat has just landed there," he said in broken English. The French continued to feign ignorance but the Dean found this exchange "a little disconcerting". They were still twenty miles from the coast – how could their plan be so widely known?

Their first attempt to be rescued ended in disaster when the motor launch was destroyed by German machine-gun fire as it arrived at the rendez-vous. They then tried, unsuccessfully, to commandeer a fishing boat that they came across on the beach. Eventually, two nights later, they found a fisherman who was willing to take them in his boat. He seemed an unlikely saviour, but he was all they had.

When darkness came, the fisherman led them down a small track between some cottages. The Dean, deciding he had used up all his luck, knelt down on the pebbly beach and prayed for success.

A cold wind whipped the waves; they could see the boat some thirty yards out bouncing in the rough surf. They waded out and found that it was already full of Italians. The boat was only big enough to carry about 25 passengers and they were more forty in total.

"What are you doing? This is our boat - we paid for it," yelled the French commandos over the noise of the sea. "So did they," said the fisherman, indicating the Italians huddled in the stern. He shrugged and smiled. There was nothing they could do; no one was going to get out. So the Dean climbed aboard and prayed once more.

In his journal, he describes a nerve wracking voyage. As they set off, the boat's engine whined and battled against the pounding surf. A couple of times it was pushed broadside to the incoming waves. The captain yelled at everyone to shift to the windward side to prevent the vessel from capsizing. For about half an hour it was unclear which would win, then slowly the noise of the surging tide began to sink into the background, the waves grew calmer and the coastline started to diminish. They had two hours of darkness left to get out of sight of land.

The Dean kept his eyes fixed on the morning star, watching it rise gracefully to take its place in the arc of the sky. He didn't want to look back. A stiff southerly wind whipped up and the captain raised the sails. Soon the east began breaking with light; the Dean looked at the mountain of the Gran Sasso shining in its new coat of snow and wondered where Richard was. At one point, a group of bombers flew low overhead in tight formation. Everyone watched them drawing the anti aircraft fire, and then there followed the explosions of their bombs, which sounded like someone pounding a table in a faraway room.

They sailed past Pescara, Ortona and the mouth of the Sangro river, all names which would become famous for their casualties in the battles that were to come in the weeks ahead. At 6pm, as the light was fading, the fisherman steered into the tiny walled harbour of Termoli.

"Very skilfully the skipper swung the boat round so that it came alongside another similar craft tied up to the steps. We scrambled out over the other craft, up the steps onto the damaged quay, free men once again."

And so ends the Dean's diary. It was Sunday November 7th 1943. The Gloomy Dean had walked back into freedom two months to the day after leaving Fontanellato.

13.

THAT SAME DAY in the hills of Carpineto forty miles inland, Richard waited anxiously. He had heard the news from the coast: that the Germans had shot up the motorboat in the bay and raided the staging area. Assuming that the Dean had been captured, he decided to abandon the sea route. The notion had been tantalising but the risk was obviously too great. He turned his back to the coast and set his mind on trying to walk through the German lines before winter froze everything in place.

It was one year since Richard had been captured in the desert. Having come this far, his overriding priority was not to get recaptured. His motto was slowly but safely – yet he could not go too slowly if he was to cross the mountains before the heavy snows arrived.

Richard had already covered well over 400 miles on foot. His boots were in a bad state of repair and his two pairs of socks were disintegrating. He had been given a vest several months ago which he now wore continuously to keep out the cold along with his battledress jacket. He estimated that Monty and the Eighth Army were only about sixty miles to the south. In fact, unknown to him, Monty's tactical HQ – the same collection of caravans and command vehicles that Richard had disappeared from a year earlier in El Alamein - was closer than that, sitting on the far bank of the Sangro river just thirty miles away.

Since the Armistice two months earlier, Monty had conquered nearly half of Italy with little opposition. The Germans had no intention of trying to defend the sparsely populated villages of the south. It was Rome that mattered to them and preventing the Alllies from breaking out to the north. The Eighth Army had breached the first of the German lines – the Volturno and the Barbara – but was now grinding to a halt on the Sangro. The Americans in the west were faring no better. After struggling to break out of their beachhead at Salerno, they had gained only 200 miles and were stuck fifty miles south of Rome on the Via Casilina.

Richard asked around among the POWs shivering in the barns and pigsties of neighbouring farms to see if anyone was willing to accompany him.

"Sure," said a South African infantry officer without cracking a smile, "I want to be back in Cape Town by Christmas."

The officer introduced himself as Jim Gill. In the ice-bound barn Richard was astonished to see that he was wearing shorts. They were made of dark blue hessian type material and looked so badly cut they could have been homemade. If he had been wearing the baggy army shorts that Eighth Army soldiers wore in the desert it would have been more understandable, but these shorts seemed utterly out of place. No contadini would ever been seen in shorts in the middle of winter in the mountains. Richard eyed them with concern.

"Always wear shorts," Jim said tersely. "I can't walk in trousers, hate the damn things." Jim Gill had grown up on a remote farm outside Paarl in the eastern Cape. He was stocky, probably no more than 5 foot 8 with sandy hair, blue eyes and a firm farmer's handshake. He didn't say much, as if he believed that words were a resource that needed careful husbanding, like water or grain. Richard sensed immediately that he shared less in common with him than he had with the donnish old Dean, but he was younger and fitter than the Dean, which was an important advantage for getting over the mountains. And besides, they didn't expect they would have to be travelling companions for very long.

The next morning, the 8th November, Richard and Jim slipped out of the farmhouse where they were staying into the freezing pre-dawn darkness. By noon they reached the dam on the Pescara river which Richard had reconnoitred two weeks before. The gate-keeper at the dam told them that many POWs had crossed this way in recent weeks; at one stage, he said, he had even kept a visitors' book though he'd thrown it away after the Germans started arriving in force. On the other side, they climbed steeply out of the valley to the lower slopes of the Majella mountains, a formidable limestone tributary of the Apennines whose peaks reached over eight and a half thousand feet and whose deep valleys had forbidding names like Vallone di Femmina Morta. The whole area was thinly inhabited and pockmarked with caves.

That winter of 1943 was particularly brutal in Italy. The snows started earlier than usual and by the first week of November, there was already several feet of snow in the passes of the Majella. In the bottom of the valleys a biting sleet set in which lasted for several weeks. In villages where food was never abundant in the best of times, there were already widespread shortages.

The women and children and elderly who made up the bulk of the population in the region had been unable to do anything to stop the German soldiers who stole the family's supplies or demanded to be fed at the family dining table. The Italian fascists had been little better; eager to show their German colleagues that they weren't soft on their own countrymen and dismissive of the rough peasants, they had taken whatever the Germans had failed to find.

The villagers had done their best to hide food in outhouses, attics and under floorboards; even burying bags of dried pasta and rice in the fields. But animals were harder to disguise and if they spotted a pig or sheep, the Germans would often herd them into the back of their trucks. The villagers were used to surrendering the occasional animal as tithe to the church but unlike the Church the Germans offered nothing in return except the threat of violence.

The families encouraged their shepherds to stay as long as they could in the high summer pastures in order to keep their flocks out of German hands. The only shelters up there were primitive huts, made out of birch branches and turf and designed for an occasional summer's night when inclement weather prevented the shepherds from sleeping outside among the leopards' bane and anemones. Some of them were made of stones, built on an ancient Greek design of the *tholos* – which involved laying flat stones one on top of the other until they met in the middle. For two days Richard and Jim climbed steadily away from the coast, stopping at farmhouses to collect as much bread as they could carry.

> *I carried only the barest essentials in the old string bag. I also carried a zappetta [a mattock] to give an air of verisimilitude – Jim carried a hatchet and bread wrapped up in a large and very dirty handkerchief. Also he seemed to be able to bestow unlimited quantities of dried figs etc in his pockets!*

Drawing of a tholos, from Richard's diary

Above Acquafredda, they stumbled across eight POWs sheltering in a cave. They had a fire at the back of the cave but it did little to dispel the cold wind. There wasn't any room for Jim and Richard so one of the prisoners led them down the hill to a *tholos*. On the way it started to sleet and they were soaking by the time they arrived.

Tuesday November 9th 1943. It had snowed in the night and was still snowing in the morning. In spite of that however, we decided to cross the pass…my boots by this time were in a pretty bad way the soles were very thin in spite of patches and the uppers cracked and in holes. But they were still boots whereas poor Jim only had thin shoes.

We plodded on, making fresh tracks in the virgin snow. It was about a foot deep on the top of the pass. There was a road down the far side and we took that as the slopes were well wooded and other routes difficult to find in the snow. About two miles from the top we came upon fresh wheel tracks and concluded that a Boche truck must have taken the wrong turning, come up so far and then turned round.

Above the village of Preturo, Richard and Jim found six more prisoners sheltering beside some cows in a hut. They were now no more than eighteen miles from Monty's headquarters: a twenty minute drive in peacetime. One of the POWs described how he had attempted to cross the Sangro River but had come across large numbers of Germans preparing defensive positions on the high ground overlooking the river. Unable to find a way round, he had turned back. In fact they had run up against the Gustav Line, the toughest and most well dug in of all of Kesselring's defensive systems.

Richard and Jim hoped that somehow they might be able to skirt between the ridgeline of the mountains and the edge of the German positions on the Sangro River.

November 10th. More rain and snow. Difficult going along the mountainside as we had to cross a number of deep ravines. When we were opposite Guardiagrele, we heard a "battle" of machine gun fire and mortars in the valley below…a local told us that some prisoners had escaped from Guardiagrele and been shot while escaping. At about 1600 hours while seated on a rock above Pennapiedimonte discussing our onward route, we saw a strange figure coming up the mountain towards us.

It was a German officer. They fled rapidly back, nearly stumbling into a chain gang of Italian soldiers digging trenches on the hill which they realized the German officer was coming up to inspect. They either had to go around the position which meant a difficult climb up into the cloud and snow of the peak or pull back to a tholos that they had passed. They decided to retreat.

That night in the hut, they shared the final tin of bully beef that Richard had carried in his knapsack all the way from Fontanellato and burrowed together under some brushwood to try to keep warm. The next morning they stuck to the tracks made by hunters and the charcoal gatherer as much as possible, but before long they found themselves approaching a main road. They could hear the sound of horses and carts but couldn't see who was driving it.

"Let's push on," said Jim impatiently. "They're bound to be Italians."

Emerging from the hedgerow they were nearly run over by a German ammunition wagon being pulled by five horses. The German soldiers slowed down and studied the two odd-looking Italian peasants as they passed a yard or so away. Richard and Jim could hear them talking; Richard was sure they were debating whether to detain them. He braced himself for the order but none came and the ammunition wagon continued to roll on down the hill. They had been saved by the Germans' inability to distinguish the fake Italian peasant from the real even when one of them was dressed in shorts.

About a mile further on, they were given a bowl of hot pasta which they ate hiding in a cowshed, as they listened to the curses of a German gun troop outside trying to manoeuvre their guns through the mud on the track a few yards away. They were surrounded by German units, and battling exhaustion. Richard had been walking for two months; one foolish mistake would undo all the time they had spent on the run. Every choice mattered now: "Everything gone but the will to hold on. Seldom had food tasted so good."

At the junction of the Lajo and Aventino rivers they encountered more gun emplacements and it wasn't until midnight that they finally found a place where they could wade across, and rewarded themselves with an hour's rest in a small hut on the other side. When they emerged, the moon had come out and in front of the hut a carpet of yellow apples glittered in the moonlight under an old tree. They jammed as many as they could into their pockets and, their spirits lifted, went on their way.

*

Around 3am they spotted an army signal cable running down the path and followed it for a while as it was the only route through the woods. Suddenly they heard someone humming ahead in the darkness. They froze. The humming stopped and through the silence came the muffled thuds of German 88mm artillery probing for the British defences on the far side of the valley.

Hardly breathing, they listened to the guns and to the silence. Then, as clearly as if they all were sitting in the same room, a field telephone rang and a German soldier suddenly stood up, no more than fifteen yards ahead of them. He stamped his boots and began talking into the phone. As far as they could tell, he was on his own, probably a sentry. Carefully lifting their feet so as not to crackle the undergrowth, Jim and Richard moved off the track back uphill into the trees.

They collapsed into a thicket of brambles, their nerves grating with tiredness and desperation. They dozed intermittently but the fear of being caught stopped them from falling asleep properly. The guns in the valley had stopped; soon it would be dawn. Unfortunately, having walked off the map that Badger Light had brought, they had little idea of their exact location.

Slowly, the sun began to penetrate the canopy of trees and warm their stiff bodies. Below them they could still hear the occasional cackle of the German sentry's radio. They wondered which direction to take. Then an explosion of noise and a boy burst through the undergrowth a few feet away. He stopped, panting heavily, and sobbing. It seemed impossible that the German sentry had not heard him.

In the noise and confusion, Jim and Richard had recoiled like animals, scrambling back into the brambles, trying to disappear. The boy seemed too preoccupied to notice. Then a few seconds later, another bigger figure appeared, holding a hunting rifle. Richard thought for a moment that the man intended to shoot the boy, but then he saw them move together, whispering. They were debating something – the man was clearly trying to calm the boy down. The two of them knelt in the undergrowth.

Richard and Jim lay there unable to move, listening to them argue as if they were watching a play. The boy looked no more than 14 years old, his face rigid with panic. Suddenly, they stood up, having clearly decided on a course of action. As they started to move off, still talking, the boy tripped on Richard's left foot.

Being taller than Jim, Richard had been unable to get his whole body inside the bramble bush. The boy stared at the strange army boot for a moment as if he had forgotten something, then grabbed hold of it and pulled fiercely. "Get up, get up," he whispered, "Who are you?" Instantly the man lifted the hunting rifle and aimed it at them, his finger on the trigger.

"*Siamo inglesi,*" said Richard rapidly. "We're English officers." Jim and Richard stood up fast, shaking off the boy's grip, to show they weren't armed.

"We're prisoners of war, we're trying to get home."

No one spoke. The two peasants eyed the fugitives warily.

"There is a German patrol coming down this path," said the man rapidly as he lowered the gun. It was all he had time to say for, as if conjuring them up, the outlines of three German soldiers appeared on the track twenty yards above them. Richard realized they were pushing a large reluctant pig ahead of them. They were waving a stick in the air to keep the pig moving forward.

The four of them immediately crouched down, Richard and Jim squatting while the two Italians knelt.

"That's our pig," fumed the teenage boy. "The bastards stole it and we're going to get it back." Despite his bravado, the boy was shaking.

Richard sucked in his breath and glanced at Jim; it was clear he was on a suicidal mission. The boy whispered rapidly into the ear of the man who raised the rifle once more to his shoulder, this time aiming it up the track at the Germans. The three young soldiers continued walking slowly towards them, slipping on the loose chalk, urging the pig on in German and chatting.

Richard shut his eyes, sickened. Having survived all this time, and just when he was so close to the end, his fate rested in the hands of a teenage boy. He had thought perhaps he would get captured and sent to Germany or shot while trying to escape, but never thought he would die in the crossfire over a stolen pig.

The Germans were now less than 20 feet away. Richard could see the insignia clearly on the collars of their jackets and their young faces under their helmets. Their attention was taken up by the pig, as it waddled from one side of the track to the other, pulling at any green leaves it could find and doing all it could to delay the journey.

As the soldiers reached the bend where the four of them lay hiding, Richard and Jim lowered their heads into the brambles. Richard could see Jim stealthily adjust his position to get ready to run and did the same.

They heard the clanking of the German's heavy backpacks and rifles as they herded the pig around the corner. Any moment now. Richard braced himself for the shot. But none came. A few seconds later the Germans had vanished. Slowly, Richard and Jim lifted their heads and stared at the two Italians in confusion. The man lowered his gun and stood up carefully.

"*Mi chiamo Antonio,*" he whispered softly and stuck out his hand. Richard took it, shaking it dumbly. The man laid a hand on the boy's shoulder.

"And this is Alfonso," he said, "my brave nephew." The man smiled and Alfonso looked a little sheepish, still panting from the adrenaline.

Richard and Jim smiled back in relief. No explanation was offered as to why they hadn't opened fire.

"Come to the farm this evening," Antonio whispered, "and we will feed you."

He pointed back up the track to a farmhouse just visible at the top of the track on the left. There was a burst of radio static from the German sentry post and the two Italians slipped away.

"Jeez," said Jim in his flat Cape accent. "That was bloody close."

*

Richard and Jim retreated to a more protected spot and debated whether to take up Antonio's offer. To stay and wait for nightfall meant a whole day sitting in damp woods. On the other hand, any movement by day now was clearly risky. They decided it was better to rest and perhaps find out more about the German positions from the family since they had clearly reached the front line.

When they went to the farmhouse that evening, however, to their disappointment the family told them little they didn't already know. The family consisted of an elderly bed–ridden father, an active mother with a severe stoop and three sons: Giovanni, Donato and Antonio – the one with the gun. In addition to them, Giovanni's wife Maria and their three sons were living with them – one of whom was Alfonso, the boy who'd tripped over Richard in the woods. Donato had one son too. In all, ten people were crowded into just two rooms, struggling to survive.

Giovanni showed Jim and Richard the hole that they had dug in the garden to hide their food from the Germans. Inside was a pitifully small pile of dried pasta, pearl barley and wheat and a few glass jars containing tomatoes. That night, however, there was no suggestion of turning the visitors away. The de Gregorios, like most contadini, had no desire to see the fascism of Mussolini replaced by a German occupation. They insisted their two guests sat in the chairs closest to the fire in the kitchen and were served first. Supper was a single ladle of pasta with a small quantity of tomato sauce.

Richard tried out his Italian with Donato, who appeared to be the most educated of the brothers and, Richard sensed, the most willing to help. Donato explained that he lived in Naples. Nervous of being conscripted by the Germans, he had come back to the family farm, bringing his seven year old son with him, though leaving his wife behind. It had clearly not been an easy decision to make.

"There's more food here than there is in the cities," he said.

"If you want to rest, you are welcome to stay here until the Allies arrive," Donato offered, implying that it was only a matter of sitting in this warm farmhouse for a few days until the Allies walked up the track. But when Richard asked him about the German presence he was less sanguine.

"Every day more German troops arrive in the area," he conceded.

After supper, Richard and Jim conferred about what to do and decided that they could not afford to stay here if the Germans were building up their troop levels in the area. Every day increased the chances of capture. Richard thanked Donato for his offer to stay but explained that they had decided to 'make a bid for it' that night. When Richard got up to say goodbye, as he had done so often before, he hoped it would be the last time they had to beg a meal.

Everyone accompanied them to the door. To Richard's dismay, the sky had cleared. The de Gregorios' tiny farmyard was filled with moonlight, throwing deep shadows under the apple trees. Richard stared at the family's handcart; he could make out every rivulet in the paintwork. The chalk track where the Germans had pushed the pig down that morning burned a bright phosphorescent white. They set off but it wasn't long before their confidence wavered; it seemed foolhardy to attempt a run to the front line in such conditions.

> *We hadn't gone far when we decided that it was taking too big a risk… so regretfully we turned back to Donato's house to accept his kind offer, believing that it would only be for a few days.*

When he and Jim reappeared at the kitchen door, Richard could see the look of fear on the de Gregorios' faces. Though they had all heard Donato's offer, they had all clearly hoped it would be declined. The family had lost their only pig that day and now, as Alfonso's mother Maria muttered bitterly, "we have to find food for two more adults."

If the Germans found them sheltering Allied officers, the farm would be burnt down and the family would lose everything. Donato was the only one who seemed genuinely delighted to see them again.

"Tonight you can sleep in the barn," he said, "but tomorrow you must go to the woods. You can sleep here at night but it is too dangerous for you to stay here in the day." The next morning they were woken by the sounds of a fierce argument. Assuming it was about them, Richard and Jim tried to make themselves inconspicuous in the small kitchen, but as he listened more, Richard realised that the family was arguing about the pig. It was Maria who had ordered Alfonso and Antonio to recover the pig. It seemed she'd been willing to risk the life of her 14 year old son for a pig, not out of affection for the animal but out of desperation. One large pig could keep a family in salami and bacon all year, but more importantly this pig had recently produced a litter of 18 piglets. She was clearly very distressed that they had failed to recover the animal.

"The babies will starve without their mother," said Maria. "One of you is going to have to go to Roccascalegna and tell the Germans that we must have the pig back." It turned out that the Germans had been collecting livestock from the surrounding farms for several weeks and bringing them to the nearby village of Roccascalegna where they had set up their headquarters. They had put up a makeshift slaughter-house and some kind of mobile canning plant which they had brought from Germany.

It was said that after the meat was canned, it was sent back to Germany where it was passed onto the divisions stumbling through the Russian snows on the Second Front.

"They will have killed it by now," mumbled Giovanni her husband, "It's too late to do anything." Maria was clearly not convinced; she turned on the men, berating them for not having the guts to get it back. Then she began pulling on her coat.

"If you are all too scared to go, I'll go," she said. No one stopped her. She marched past Richard and Jim without even acknowledging them and disappeared out of the door.

After breakfast, Alfonso said he knew a cave in the woods where he'd played where they could spend the day. The idea made Richard's heart sink; he thought of all those POWs he'd encountered sitting in caves waiting to be rescued.

The boy raced in front, rejuvenated by his new mission. Ten minutes later he was calling softly to them from the top of an outcrop of rock. The 'cave' turned out to consist of six giant boulders which lay one on top of each other in a ragged pyramid. In between, where saplings and brambles had grown up, was a dark slit of an opening which you could only reach by clambering up the side of one boulder and peering over the lip.

The slit slanted down a steep angle between the boulders, appearing to go right into the heart of the pyramid. High bushes obscured the entrance so that it was invisible unless you actually knew what you were looking for. Above it stood a small promontory of rock which rose out of the trees like a bulbous forehead.

As they pushed their way in Richard and Jim realised the slit

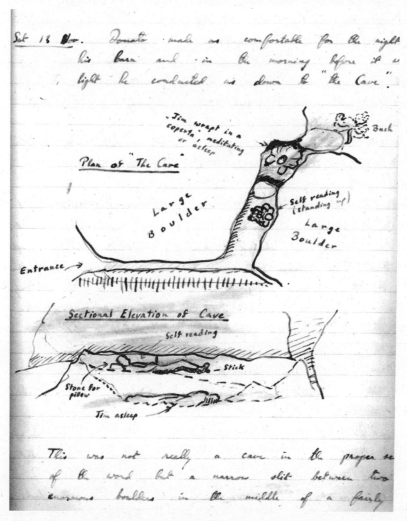

Cross-section of the cave, drawn by Richard

did a sharp left turn around a boulder. They could see daylight at the other end; if needed perhaps they could get out that way in an emergency by clambering over a thick bush. The disadvantage, as they soon discovered, was that the cave was not waterproof. The limestone rock was porous and during heavy downpours water would drip through in several places as well as pour down the sides of the boulders.

Before he left, Alfonso pointed out the German signal cable, the same one that Richard and Jim had stumbled upon, running along the bottom of the valley less than a hundred metres away.

"It's the Germans' main communication between their front line and the rear area on this part of the battlefront. And it's well guarded," he warned, "though the sentry seems to have gone."

Glumly, Richard and Jim moved in.

"I hate the idea of staying still," said Richard.

"It'll only be for a couple of days," Jim reassured him, "until the moon has waned."

14.

"So beg'an the long and tedious period of waiting…" Richard wrote. The next few days passed very slowly. Richard missed the Dean and his easy stream of chatter and observations. Though he felt sure that Jim wouldn't hesitate to risk his life for him if he had to, he showed little interest in wanting to talk. The floor of the cave was full of rocky debris leaving limited space to lie down. Jim spent hours crouching silently on his haunches, either meditating or asleep under his army poncho. The Italians called him "basso" due to his short stocky frame and were amazed at how he continued to wear shorts like a South African farmer on all but the coldest days.

Every evening they would go up to the farmhouse where they were given supper by the family before walking across the yard to the barn to fall asleep. Donato gave them some paper and pencils that he had kept from Naples to while away the time in the cave. Richard wrote lists: everyone he was with in camp, everyone he could remember from Charterhouse, all the books he had read, all the saints he knew. When he had exhausted that, he invented crossword puzzles which he would offer to Jim to solve.

Jim's favourite game was to draw up categories of things and choose a letter and write down birds beginning with R or capital cities beginning with S. Jim always won the nature questions while Richard won history and current affairs.

Years later, I would come to know this as "the geography game": pieces of paper would be handed round the family every Christmas time, and everyone would take it in turns to suggest a category then someone would open a book at random and with eyes closed, put their finger on a letter. We had 15 minutes to names as many plants, trees, countries, rivers, mountains, prime ministers as we could. My father seemed to have a limitless supply of names of rivers; only later did it occur to me that he might have learnt them from Jim. Once I suggested football teams as a category but was firmly told that was inappropriate.

*

The days passed monotonously and with little incident. Sometimes they saw Allied planes pass overhead and the German guns round about would open up. Sometimes they heard bombing or artillery coming from the Allied lines. They had only one book in English: Aunt Bulley's New Testament that Richard had faithfully carried in his knapsack from camp.

In the evenings, Donato came and took them from the cave back to his home where they would get warm by the fire and have a good meal of *minestra*, then smoke and chat with him by the fire until retiring to the barn and their bed of straw.

Gradually the family adjusted to the presence of the men. On the third evening they noticed, when they went to bed in the barn, that the old sow had reappeared, surrounded by her large squealing litter. Maria had a large smile on her face. Astonished, Richard asked what had happened. Maria, good as her word, had walked to Roccascalegna and demanded an audience with the German commander. She had explained that his soldiers had taken a pig which had just given birth to 18 pig-

174

lets and if he returned the pig, she would be able to give him not one but several pigs in the next few months to support the brave troops fighting in Russia. The German commander accepted the undeniable logic of the proposition and ordered the pig to be released.

Richard and Jim never made a conscious decision to stay in the cave – it just happened incrementally. Each day brought another reason not to move – bad weather, reports from the village of large numbers of German troops manoeuvring, radio reports which showed that the English army had been unable to advance across the Sangro.

The de Gregorios did not possess a radio but they would bring news back of the Eighth Army from listening to Radio Bari in neighbours' houses. Richard often wondered if Monty had any idea where he was. A year had passed since he had disappeared. And he assumed that, while Monty had known that he was in Fontanellato, he may now no longer believe he was alive.

In fact, Monty was doing all he could to find out what had happened to his stepson and had a pretty good sense of what was going on. He had now set up his headquarters at Paglieta on the southern bank of the Sangro, which was 10 miles by crow's flight from Richard's cave. A slow trickle of POWs continued to arrive there from the north. And Monty had given orders that all Allied POWs who came across the frontline be questioned about his stepson's whereabouts.

"I have had several bits of news from escaped prisoners about Dick Carver," Monty wrote on 20th November 1943 to the Reynolds. "I think there is no doubt he is at large and is hanging about waiting for our advance to over-run the place he is in. If my information is correct he is somewhere just north of the Pescara river, he must have walked a long way as I think his camp was up somewhere in Northern Italy in the Po valley. It would be a grand thing if we can rescue him before Xmas. You might let Mrs Bailey know the above news; also Mrs Mather."

As time went on, Richard became increasingly fond of Donato. Having lived in Naples, Donato had a much broader understanding of the war and the world than most of the contadini. Richard looked forward to each evening when they could walk up through the woods to the farmhouse and sit by the fire. Donato would tell stories about Naples and sometimes sing Neapolitan stories in a soft tuneful voice.

Donato was very good company, Not deeply religious but a sincere liberalist and humanitarian. Though a native of Abruzzo he talked beautiful Italian.

Richard was a firm Anglican, a believer not only in Christ but in the rituals of the church. He was surprised to find that Donato's atheism didn't bother him. One evening he confided in Donato about who his stepfather was.

"It's better the family does not know this," Donato said. "it will only make them more frightened and more reluctant to let you stay."

Richard could see that Donato was having difficulty persuading his brothers that they should continue to look after the two fugitives. But Donato clearly longed to make some contribution to beating the Germans since he was not fighting, and here was an opportunity that fate had given him. He was determined to get Richard and Jim home safely, especially since they had come so far.

Donato professed himself disgusted with his own people who had not had the spirit to rebel against Mussolini's yoke and he always said that he intended to go out to the Argentine after the war and start afresh. I used to tell him that his duty was to his own people and that he was the kind of man who would be needed to rebuild post-war Italy and personally I think he will stay and go into politics.

On the morning of November 21st as he accompanied them back through the woods to the cave, Donato said he had told their family doctor, Doctor Cucchini, about what they were doing.

"He has a house in the village but at the moment he is hiding somewhere nearby because he is afraid he will be recruited by the Germans into the army. It's important he knows about you in case you get sick."

Richard sensed that Donato was anticipating that they were going to stay for a while. He paused and pointed across the valley at a small white house standing on its own on the road leading out of Roccascalegna.

"Do you see that house? That's the house of Doctor Cucchini's mistress. From there she can see anyone leaving or entering the village. If she sees a German patrol heading this way, she lowers a sheet out of that window above her front door. That's a signal to us to make sure you are back in the cave and not at the farmhouse."

*

In the third week of November it started raining heavily and did not stop for ten days. The Sangro river swelled to twice its normal size, flooding the fields for hundreds of yards on either side. In places the icy cold river was 100 feet deep. Ten miles away at Paglieta, Monty grilled his meteorologists, desperate for a break in the weather. The pontoon bridges that the Royal Engineers had put in place had all been swept away; all the tracks in the area had turned into treacherous run-offs of mud and icy slush.

A couple of weeks earlier, disaster had struck Monty's camp. Monty's artillery chief had been captured while he was reconnoitring possible crossing points on the river. The German patrol had seized several of his maps which showed the points on the Gustav Line where Monty intended to attack. Kesselring the

Donato de Gregorio

German commander immediately pushed more troops into the area to reinforce the high ground on the north bank. Monty realized that he was not going to be able to cross the river on multiple fronts. Instead he focused all his resources on extending and holding a single bridgehead. But getting even a few units across the monstrous torrent under enemy fire was a long slow process.

That night the Germans used flame-throwers and tanks to try to prevent the Allies from establishing any kind of bridgehead on the northern bank of the river. But with the help of repeated air raids by the RAF, Monty's forces slowly dislodged the Germans from the high ground and they were able to establish a permanent footing on the north bank. The Gustav Line was beginning to crack.

"Many were drowned. Eventually we succeeded," Monty wrote on 27th November.

Unaware of the Allies' progress, Richard became more and more downcast. The continual rain made it impossible to stay dry in the cave. He and Jim crouched under the overhangs trying to find patches where the water did not come through. They scratched at the growing colonies of lice on their bodies.

Donato said the wireless reported that Allied troops were fighting in the Sangro valley below Altino… Tomorrow we might be free.

But it didn't happen.

17th, 18th, 19th, 20th, 21st, 22nd: days pass. 23rd: got rather depressed.

Depressed is not a word my father used lightly. But it seems at this point that he really began to lose heart. He and Jim started to believe they were not going to make it; that they were going to be recaptured right at the finish line. They felt as imprisoned as they had felt in POW camp – they were trapped in a wood surrounded by thousands of German troops with winter closing in. Occasionally, Richard wondered whether they should try to "disappear" into the countryside, but Jim had no interest in such a plan. He remained as determined as ever to get home.

One morning Richard was sitting outside the cave, encouraging the feeble November sun to dry his clothes from another night of rain, when he spotted four German soldiers coming down the other side of the valley. They were walking purposefully through the bushes straight towards them, a couple of Alsatian dogs straining at their leashes.

The patrol paused and Richard watched as the leader appeared to point straight at the cave. What had happened to the doctor's mistress and the early warning system? Where were Donato and the others? Had the family been arrested? Richard ducked down and waited until the Germans reached the stream at the bottom of the valley less than a hundred metres away where for a few seconds they disappeared out of sight. He ran back inside the cave to warn Jim.

Rather than crouch at the back of the cave, they decided to hide right underneath the small entrance so that anyone peering in might look over their heads and not spot them. It was a forlorn chance and if they were spotted there was no possibility of escape.

They could hear the dogs panting as the patrol moved relentlessly up the slope towards them. One of the soldiers swished at the undergrowth just outside the cave with a stick. It was such an ordinary sound, as if he had dropped something and was looking for it. Any moment now Richard was certain the Germans would look up and notice the curious slit in the rock a few feet away. Then, from right above their heads, he heard one of the Germans call out in a mixture of Italian and English: "*Venite, venite, buono Americano,* we are your friends."

The soldiers were now standing on the boulder directly above the cave, less than fifteen feet from them. Jim and Richard crouched as low as possible. Richard hoped that he had not left any of his clothes drying on the bushes; from that vantage point it seemed certain that they would notice there were signs of human activity around the cave. But after a few minutes, the noises subsided, and eventually they could hear the leader of the section barking orders further down the valley.

Richard crept on his stomach around the boulder and peered through the bush. He could see four grey uniforms retreating into the distance. Immediately, they put all their provisions into their pockets in case they needed to make a run for it.

For the remainder of the day the soldiers stayed at the far end of the valley, watched by two pairs of hidden eyes. They seemed to be waiting for something to happen. When darkness fell, a sentry appeared on the track just below the farmhouse in the same spot where Alfonso had stumbled over Richard's foot two weeks before. It was as if they knew the route Richard and Jim took to reach the family each night.

Long before midnight I had given up all hope of Donato coming and resigned myself to a miserable night. I shall never forget the feeling of relief and joy when I heard the slight sounds of his approach and saw his shadowy form through the bushes and then the final proof that it was he, his whispered 'Dick, Jim'. Ever after that I knew that we could trust him absolutely.

Donato explained how he and Alfonso had attempted to reach the cave earlier, but had run into the German sentry on the track. He led them back on a different path to the farmhouse avoiding the track. In the kitchen, they found the entire family on edge. Giovanni and Antonio were claiming they could still hear the Germans moving around in the valley.

"If the Germans find out what we are doing, this farm will be burnt down," said Giovanni. "Even if they don't kill us, we will have lost everything."

"It's our duty to protect them," retorted Donato. No one looked at the two prisoners standing silently near the fire.

"For you Donato, it is easy to say," replied Giovanni. "Your wife is not here and your house is not here. And what about the little ones? We have to think of them."

The brothers thought someone in the village had betrayed them, which was why the Germans had searched the woods.

"Otherwise how else would they have known?" said Donato. "They are fully committed trying to fight the British, they don't have time to look for escaped POWs – unless they know where they are hiding. Someone told them."

*

Sitting outside the cave a few days later on the morning of November 26th, Jim spotted two German soldiers pulling up the signal line that ran along the valley floor. Finally, this was some tangible proof that the Germans were pulling back. Later that day Donato

arrived to say that the Germans appeared to be leaving Roccascalegna.

Their spirits lifted. That evening, instead of going to the farmhouse as usual, Donato took Richard and Jim up to Roccascalegna
to visit his friend, Doctor Cucchini. The three of them entered the
village without incident. The doctor described how the Germans
had evacuated the entire village within six hours that morning. In
the afternoon he had managed to walk back into his own house.
They found him in his cellar, complaining about the number of
bottles of wine the Germans had stolen in his absence, though
he was still able to produce several bottles which they used to celebrate the enemy's departure.

> *The doctor bemoans the loss of his best wine, some furniture and*
> *even tablecloths and cutlery which the Germans have taken. But*
> *he seems to have a good deal left and he gave a very good lunch....*
> *From the upper windows of his house one gets a glorious view of the*
> *snow covered Majella mountains. I tried to get into the old castello;*
> *but in a fit of pique the Boche before they left had shot away the lock*
> *and one couldn't open the gate.*

Just to be able to walk around the village made Richard light-
headed with euphoria. When they returned to the cave that afternoon, he and Jim got ready for the final sprint, repairing their
shoes and making sure they had a few provisions to carry in their
pockets. Everywhere the mood began to lighten; people felt that
they might survive the war after all. They could even begin to plan
a future.

Donato's brother, Antonio, decided to celebrate the Germans'
retreat by proposing to a girl that he known since school who lived
in the nearby village of Gessopalena. He was the only one of the
three brothers not yet married and his parents approved of the
match, giving him their blessing to go to the village and make his
offer.

The next day Antonio set out. Alfonso accompanied him but halfway there he turned around, saying that he had left something behind. Antonio went on alone, his mind full of a future that lay far away from the farmhouse and the war. When he reached the girl's house, she was standing by the window waiting for him. As they stood talking awkwardly in the doorway, a formation of British Lancaster bombers rumbled overhead. On a map somewhere in Monty's headquarters, the area around Roccascalegna had been highlighted as a target. The British had no idea that the Germans had left.

There was a deafening roar, and the door lintel fell in, missing the girl but landing on Antonio and pinning him to the ground. Semi-conscious, he was carried back down the track by her family. He appeared not to have broken anything more serious than his leg, but he was delirious and incoherent. It took a day for Doctor Cucchini to reach him. He diagnosed meningitis, brought on by the incident. Without antibiotics there was nothing he could do, and three days later Antonio was dead. Antonio, the youngest brother who had resisted firing at the Germans and who had first extended hospitality to two unknown Allied officers, had been killed by an Allied bomb.

"And just at the moment he was about to propose," said Donato. "At least we hope that he died happy."

Richard felt culpable. It was a heavy burden of grief to carry for a family who had already endured so much. Donato asked Richard and Jim if they would take him with them across the front line. He'd decided to try to get back to his home in Naples which was now in Allied hands. He said he would have to wait for Antonio's funeral, and Richard agreed to wait with him.

Jim, impatient to get back to South Africa, decided to leave immediately take his chance of crossing the frontline alone. They said goodbye outside the cave and Richard watched him walk down into the valley and up the other side. He had his shorts on once more, confident he would be on the Allied side by darkness.

Five months later Richard received a letter from South Africa – he had made it back to Paarl in time for Christmas.

*

On the day after Antonio's funeral, the rains that had fallen for the past two weeks finally stopped. "It is a glorious sunny day and my spirits are high," Richard wrote in his diary. The Germans had vanished, and Richard realized that they must now be in a sort of no-man's-land between the two armies.

It took him and Donato less than an hour to reach the Sangro. The signs of battle were everywhere; abandoned trenches, upturned vehicles and artillery guns lay either side of the road, the houses along the river bank had been flattened by the British shelling. Just north of Bomba, the main road to the coast and the railway line crossed the river, but both the bridges had been blown by the retreating Germans.

Donato and Richard stood despondently on the bank, watching the debris-strewn torrent rushing through the broken arches. They didn't know it but they had hit the river at a place on the frontline in between two battles. Had they walked ten miles downstream they would have run straight into fierce fighting between Monty's 2nd New Zealand Division and Kesselring's forces. The New Zealanders had managed to establish a bridgehead on the north bank of the river, but the Germans were throwing wave after wave of troops against them to stop them breaking out into the coastal plain. A few miles upstream under the Majella mountains, Monty's 5th Division was also attempting to cross the Sangro and encircle the German positions from behind.

A crossing looked near impossible. And then Richard noticed that, although the railway bridge had been blown up, the track was still intact, hanging in giant loops of twisted iron between the shattered concrete pillars.

"If we sit on one rail and put our feet on the other we might just be able to creep across like crabs," he said.

Donato looked dubious. It was a long way – they could count at least ten arches in the bridge and at several points the rail was almost touching the cresting water. "What if it gives way while we are on it?"

"We don't have much choice," said Richard. He went first, edging out over the river, but Donato stayed on the bank refusing to move.

"I can't do it," he said above the noise of the water.

Richard went out a bit further to show Donato that the rails were secure and able to take their weight. Then he came back.

After protesting more, Donato finally sat down on the left rail and put his feet gingerly onto the other. "Don't look down," said Richard.

Holding on tightly, Donato began to cross. Richard staying close to him, encouraging and cajoling him forwards. Apart from the distant sound of artillery exchange down the valley, there was no sign of any military, either German or Allied. It hardly felt that they were crossing a frontline. As they approached the middle of the river, Richard turned his face up to the sun and smiled – he had done it. He could stop running and hiding. He lifted one hand and cheered to Donato, then lost his balance and nearly toppled over into the foam.

It was mid-afternoon when they walked into an American headquarters on the outskirts of Atessa. The American guards were startled when Richard told them that they were the first Allied position they had reached – they had thought that they were in the rear area and that there was a large number of British troops in front of them. The Americans took them to a corner of a farmyard where a number of other escaped prisoners sat around a couple of ammunition boxes that served as a table. They wore a curious variety of army uniform and peasants' clothing and the shoes of several of them had disintegrated. The Americans gave them some rations and they celebrated with tea and English cigarettes. They didn't talk about their experiences, preferring just to enjoy the moment, a private victory in a long war. Richard noticed the other escapees eyeing Donato suspiciously.

"He's on his way back to see his family in Naples," Richard said and explained briefly how his family had sheltered him and Jim.

American razors, cigarettes and soap arrived for the POWs, all of which Richard quietly passed on to Donato. He sensed Donato's nervousness. Crossing the frontline had reversed their roles. Richard could see that it was now Donato who was dependent on him. He was a refugee in his own country who now had to navigate his way through the detritus of war. His position was ambiguous; half of his country was on one side of the war, half still on the other. He was afraid of being ensnared by the Allied war machine that was slowly grinding its way up Italy.

A cage of German POWs marched past the farmyard under the watchful eye of a New Zealand military policeman; it was the first time Richard had seen any German prisoners. The balance of war, he reflected, had tipped from this time a year ago when he had been marched by the Germans to the transport plane at Sollum.

Richard asked one of the American officers if Monty's headquarters were nearby.

"Why do you want to know?" the American asked.

"I'm his stepson," replied Richard.

The American looked at him coolly and then called over a British liaison officer from the Eighth Army. The officer who had been in the desert recognised Richard and confirmed that he was Monty's stepson.

"You want to go and see him?" the American asked, suddenly smiling.

"Yes, please."

Richard stayed the night with the New Zealanders and Donato managed to locate a friend in the town who gave him a bed.

The next morning Richard gave Donato a travel pass allowing him to travel on military transport to Naples. He was effusive in his gratitude, though Richard knew that the flimsy piece of paper written by an American warrant officer was scant repayment for all the risks Donato had taken to protect him.

They said goodbye standing in the street. Richard did not make close friends easily. In the most unlikely circumstances, he had encountered someone with a similar gentle, tolerant attitude to life like his own. He admired Donato's compassion and felt happy in his company. They promised to meet up again as soon as the war allowed it, though Richard gave little indication in his diary that he thought it would actually happen. He was more realistic, perhaps, about how much separated them.

15.

RICHARD WAS GIVEN a shower, and a shave and a new set of uniform. The British liaison officer offered to drive him the six miles downstream to Monty's tactical HQ at Paglieta.

Sitting in the back, upright, cleanshaven and combed, chatting politely to the officer and his driver, Richard realized that his life on the road was over. He had left behind his farmer's trousers and his *zappetta* at the American headquarters and his new uniform felt awkward and unfamiliar. He had no idea how much other elements in his life had shifted since he had been away.

When Richard had been captured, his stepfather had been a relatively obscure British general, one among many. One year later Monty had become a familiar name in every household in the Empire. The propaganda film of the North African campaign, "Desert Victory", had been played in countless darkened Gaumonts and Odeons. The publicity shot of Monty leaning out of his tank turret, his foxy angular face craning forward with his binoculars round his neck had become one of the most recognizable images of the war.

As Richard stepped out of the jeep, he was told that Monty was just finishing a briefing in the mess tent. He waited by the car. A few minutes later, Monty came out. He was dressed in a typically unorthodox outfit of a fleece-lined bomber's jacket, a jersey, no tie and wearing his trademark black beret with two cap badges.

"Where the hell have you been?" he said, looking stern for a moment before breaking into a grin.

Monty must have been warned that Richard was on his way up from the American HQ for he'd arranged for an official photographer to be present. They shook hands as a group of Monty's staff surrounded them and applauded.

"What took you so long?" said Monty, clapping Richard on the shoulder. "Had Carol Mather through here several weeks ago." The put-down was typical of Monty who found it impossible to cede the limelight gracefully even for a few moments. But when I look at the photographs of them standing together beside Monty's caravan, the light in Monty's eyes is obvious and his smile is real. He looks relieved – he is a father who has recovered his son.

Richard clearly felt his joy. "Monty was obviously delighted to see me," he wrote in his diary, "and started making jokes about my clothes."

He took Richard on a tour of his Tac HQ, showing him off to his aides and camp followers. They walked around Monty's collection of canaries and lovebirds as the official photographer clicked away and Monty explained how he had reluctantly given up the peacock that had travelled with him all the way up Italy after it had bitten two of his ADCs.

"Gave it away to a local farmer, who ate it if he had any sense."

After dinner, he took Richard through his plan of attack, describing how he was going to "knock Kesselring and the German army for six right out of Italy" as soon as he was able to cross the Sangro. To Richard, Monty seemed to be the same bustling, self-confident, dogmatic, energetic person, except that his traits seemed

Richard and Monty, posing for photographs outside Monty's
caravans at Tac HQ, Paglieta, on 4th December 1943

to have been magnified by his fame - as if in his mind success had somehow justified his mood swings, his staggering tactlessness and equally startling kindnesses.

He presented Richard with a signed copy of his "Personal Message to the Troops" which he had read out three days earlier to a large gathering of soldiers from every frontline unit.

"The Allies have conquered about one-third of Italy since we invaded the country on 3rd September," it read. "But the Germans still hold the approaches to Rome, and that city itself… WE WILL NOW HIT THE GERMANS A COLOSSAL CRACK. Good luck to you all. And good hunting as we go forward."

Monty had arranged for a bed for Richard to be made up in his map-room caravan and told him how the caravan had been captured from an Italian general after the battle of El Alamein who was now the Minister of War in the Badoglio government and therefore on the Allied side.

"But if he thinks he's getting his caravan back, he's not!" he shouted, chortling away.

That night, after retiring to his own caravan Monty wrote to the Reynoldses, "5th December – Dick Carver has just come in. He is very well, but is thin and wants feeding up I should say. I shall send him home at once… it will be nice for him to be home for Christmas."

*

Richard's reappearance was a rare moment of happiness for Monty. Underneath the usual bluster he was becoming increasingly anxious and fretful. His army was grounded in the mud. Having pushed the enemy back from El Alamein 1800 miles, all the way along the north African coast, through Sicily and up the Adriatic coast, he was now stuck.

But it wasn't only having his progress halted that chafed at Monty. He was afraid that his star was about to be eclipsed. Among the senior ranks of the British army, it was now an open secret that

**Monty showing Richard his collection of
love-birds**

Roosevelt and the Americans were turning their attention away
from Italy and the southern Mediterranean and focusing on an
invasion in Northern Europe. As all eyes turned north, Monty
could tell that the Italian front was becoming less important. His
requests for additional troops and tanks were starting to fall on
deaf ears.

In early November, the idea of invading northern Europe
had acquired a code name – Operation Overlord – with General

EIGHTH ARMY

PERSONAL MESSAGE FROM THE ARMY COMMANDER

To be read out to all Troops

1.   The Allies have conquered about one-third of ITALY since we invaded the country on 3rd September. But the Germans still hold the approaches to ROME, and that city itself.

2.   The time has now come to drive the Germans north of ROME. The Eighth Army is not advancing on the direct ROME axis; it is the Fifth American Army which is on that line. But our help is vital if the Fifth Army is to secure ROME. And we will do our part in a manner worthy of the best traditions of the Eighth Army and the Desert Air Force.

3.   The enemy has been outfought by better troops ever since we first landed in SICILY, and his men don't like what they are getting.

     The Germans are in fact in the very condition in which we want them.

     WE   WILL NOW HIT THE GERMANS A COLOSSAL CRACK.

4.   Good luck to you all. And good hunting as we go forward.

B. L. MONTGOMERY
General,
Eighth Army.

25 November, 1943.
ITALY,

Eisenhower as its supreme commander. On 29th November, during their meeting in Tehran, Stalin had surprised Churchill by asking who was going to command the land forces in the operation. Assuming that Russia wanted to be involved, Churchill had started mumbling about how the three powers could decide collectively, to which Stalin replied that he simply wanted to know.

Since an American was the supreme commander, it was likely that a British general would get the post of commanding the land forces – an appointment which would be the crowning achievement of any career; a chance to makes amends for the debacle of Dunkirk, to restore British pride and honour and demonstrate Britain's superiority in the league of European nations.

By early December, when Richard arrived at Paglieta, Monty knew that his rival, General Harold Alexander, was being favoured for the job by both Eisenhower and Churchill. Alex and Monty were almost exact contemporaries. Though Alex was four years younger, they had been promoted generals within months of each other and had both commanded corps during the retreat from Dunkirk. As the commander-in-chief for the British forces in the Middle East, Alex was Monty's commanding officer. However, since El Alamein Monty had become much the more famous general of the two.

Alexander was the antithesis of Monty in both temperament and background, the third son of the 4th Earl of Caledon from County Tyrone in Ireland. He had shown great courage in the First World War as a junior officer, and viewed the military life with an aristocrat's cool detachment, utterly different to the emotional fury that Monty brought to the task. While Monty was constantly riding his subordinates to change tactics, Alex left his commanders to fight their battles in the way they wanted.

Monty studied obsessively and pushed and elbowed his way up the ranks; Alex used his charm for advancement. He was close to Churchill and, like the Prime Minister, had attended Harrow and Sandhurst. Churchill was convinced that Alex's smooth diplomatic skills would be essential for handling the Americans. The war was quickly becoming a joint operation between the two nations and political tact and judgment were increasingly necessary skills.

But once again General Alan Brooke, the Chief of the Imperial General Staff, saw things differently. He believed that the most important quality for commanding the vast coalition of land forces in Operation Overlord was going to be the ability to think strategically, and he had little faith in Alexander's abilities to do that.

"Alex, charming as he is, fills me with gloom," Brooke wrote in his diary, "He cannot see big... He will never have either the personality or the vision to command three services."

From his caravan on the damp banks of the Sangro, Monty lobbied furiously for the position, scribbling letters to Lord Mountbatten in Asia, the Reynoldses in England, his former field commanders scattered across the battlefield and to anyone else who would listen, trying to shift the decision in his favour. He had no qualms about openly undermining his rival.

"Alexander is a very great friend of mine and I am very fond of him," he wrote on one occasion. "But I am under no delusion whatsoever as to his ability to conduct large scale operations in the field."

"The higher art of making war is beyond him," he wrote to another colleague. "We are on a very good wicket now and we have the winning of the war in our pocket – but if we make mistakes, and don't put the right men in the right place, we shall merely prolong the whole business."

In mid-December, the 69-year-old Churchill was struck down with pneumonia and took himself off to Tunis to recuperate. For a few crucial days, Alex was without his most powerful advocate. This may have been the factor which tipped the decision Monty's way. Brooke succeeded in lining up the War Cabinet behind Monty and made a formal recommendation to the Prime Minister. Churchill, too exhausted to overrule Brooke, gave in, and on 23rd December

SUBJECT   STANDING COMMITTEE OF ADJUSTMENT

REF. & DATE   O2S/1116CA/D494   23rd May 45

FROM ___   GHQ, 2nd Echelon, MEF

TO   WAR OFFICE (REGISTRY), LONDON, S.W.1.

SHEET

1/1

The following report relating to the affairs of

Major R. O. H. CARVER, Royal Engineers, posted HQ. Eighth Army

who was a prisoner of war, is submitted in conformance with WOINDOC ref. 45/Gen/5556 AG1a) dated 17th May, 1944, para. 10(b).

1.   Casualty :-   Reported missing 7th November, 1942, in the Western Desert - Middle East Daily Casualty List No.428.
Confirmed prisoner of war - Middle East Daily Casualty List No.479, dated 30th January, 1943.
Reported safe, recovered from enemy hands - Middle East Daily Casualty List No.780, dated 17th January, 1944.

2.   Next of kin : -   No record

3.   Effects : -   The following is an extract of a letter received from Main HQ, Eighth Army, at the time of the casualty : -

"Major R.O.H. Carver, RE, was captured with his Staff Car during a move of this HQ.

All his belongings were in his car at the time and consequently nothing is left here to dispose of."

The pieces described below were collected from Thos. Cook & Son, Ltd., Cairo, on the 13th May 1943 : -

1 black tin trunk   1 white wooden box
1 shotgun in a case   1 black kitbag
1 white kitbag   1 camp bed
1 roll

The white kitbag was salvaged and the contents transferred to the other pieces.   The shotgun, the camp bed and the roll were packed in the tin trunk.   3 pieces, viz :-

1 white wooden box   1 black kitbag   1 tin trunk

were forwarded on the 15th May, 1943 to Cox & Kings, Liverpool, (Inventories were enclosed in each piece)

4.   Monetary assets:-   No monetary assets of Major Carver were received by the Committee.

Barclays Bank (DC&O) Cairo, have informed the Committee that they hold an account lying dormant in the name of this officer.

5.   Claims : -   No claims against the officer were received.

(R.H. NICOLLS) Major,
President,   Standing
Committee of Adjustment,
GHQ. 2nd Echelon. MEF.

1943, the telegram arrived at Monty's HQ in Paglieta, ordering him home to command the land forces in Operation Overlord.

Richard had started for home a fortnight earlier, after enduring three nights in Monty's cold and leaky caravan. It often took months for the cumbersome bureaucracy of the army to get former POWs back to Britain, but Monty had fast-tracked him, making sure he received VIP treatment along the way. He wrote to the Reynoldses:

"I have sent Dick Carver off by air and he should have reached England before you get this. We enjoyed having him here and I was glad to be able to satisfy myself that he is alright – physically and mentally. We were photographed together a great deal and an American cinema man took 'shots' of us; so we may appear together on the films!!"

Richard's first stop was Bari, the same port where he had experienced his first taste of imprisonment in the transit camp, and where now, ironically, he stayed as a guest of General Alexander, oblivious to all the machinations that were going on about Operation Overlord. From there, he was flown on to Algiers where he was put up in "a sumptuous guest house" at Allied Forces Headquarters, then on through Oran and Marrakesh, finally arriving in the UK on Sunday 12th December 1943.

Of the 80,000 British soldiers that were in Italian prisoner of war camps the day the Italian Armistice was signed, only one in seven made it all the way home. But Richard was characteristically modest about his achievement. The entire entry for Sunday 12th December 1943 reads:

Arrived at Prestwick 1000 hours. Home again after 6 years!

16.

IT IS SEPTEMBER before I get the chance to visit my father again
from America. This time I bring my six-year-old son, Jude.

My father still lives in the same house on the south coast of
England which he and my mother retired to in the Eighties. It sits
a hundred yards from the village church behind a straggly hedge
that has grown up unbidden and now acts as the primary division
of the property. The house was built in the 1920s out of concrete
with a layer of white pebbledash to give it a false veneer of gentility.
When my parents moved in they did little to renovate it beyond putting up some rather odd floral wallpaper in the dining room which
my mother had acquired in a January sale; it was only enough to
cover half of one wall and my mother never found another rem-
nant to match it. She bought off-cuts of carpet and linoleum from
the local furnishing stores which vied with the rugs brought back
by my father from Persia, Kashmir, India and Jordan – the distant
outposts of the British Empire where he had once lived.

After lunch, Jude asks if he can ride a bike along the seafront.
In the garage I discover my old Raleigh, still covered in the defiant

Richard Carver, with his grandson Jude

red that I painted it when I was seven. I was obsessed with pirates at the time and loved the Raleigh's brass plaque that stood out below the handlebars like the figurehead of a galleon. Summer after summer it has sat forgotten behind the lawn mower.

A fierce westerly wind chases Jude around the seafront car park while Dad and I sit in his car watching him. The rubber of the rear tyre has almost disintegrated, but Jude doesn't seem to mind. I wonder about my father and how close he came to being killed in the war. Was it luck or good judgment that had held him back from leaping off that German truck in the desert and trying to escape into the night? I imagine the young German lieutenant raising his pistol. Then the modest crack of the shot, and Richard's life draining away into the wet sand.

As I gaze at the seagulls floating on the wind, I try to imagine the lives that never happened of men my father knew: the children they never had, the love affairs and careers that never developed – I wonder if he still feels their absence.

After he turned ninety, my siblings and I prevailed on our

father to allow a carer to live with him. For a long time he bristled at the idea of having a stranger in his home. He insisted that he could still get upstairs on his own, but eventually confessed that he sometimes crawled up on his hands and knees.

Miriam, a gentle Trinidadian woman from east London, is looking after him at the moment. The next morning at breakfast I find that she and my father have arranged to go on a shopping expedition – although it turns out that Miriam herself cannot drive. "Don't worry," she says cheerfully, "We've been going out every day. He's a good driver."

The nearest town is only fifteen minutes away by car but after three hours they have still not returned. I have long since finished lunch when I eventually hear the sound of wheels on the gravel drive. They'd spent an hour and a half driving around the outskirts of Southampton unable to find a way out. I start to tell Miriam how dangerous it is having him drive but she cuts me off.

"We make a fine pair, don't we?" she says, rolling the don't in her Trinidadian accent. "But when you're old there's nothing to rush back to, you know." I study my father for signs of concern but he seems perfectly cheerful. In fact he seems to have enjoyed the experience.

"By the way," says Miriam, "when we were in the car trying to find our way out, he told me that he once got lost driving around in the Sahara desert."

She seems to think he was making it up.

*

The war did not stop for my father after he returned from Italy that December. Six months later, he was driving a tracked troop carrier off a landing craft into the shallow waters of the Normandy beaches amid the chaos of burnt out vehicles and hundreds of thousands of troops assembling. During the fighting in northern France he would have dinner occasionally with Monty at his headquarters, always leaving with armfuls of cigarettes for his troops.

One morning, as he was driving in his jeep near Caen, a mortar exploded nearby. A shell fragment passed through his right leg just above the ankle, shattering the bones and creating the indentation that used to fascinate me as a child. He was flown back to England on a stretcher. While he was in the convalescent home, he received a letter from Italy.

Naples, December 5, 1944

Dearest Dich

I am back in Naples today only and I can't tell you how pleased I was to find in my Office your letter of 29/8.

I hope that by now your leg has perfectly recovered and that you are not looking for more fun in stopping other German bullets.

If and when you will return to Italy, you know very well that here there are two brotherly arms, a heart and a house always open to you and to whoever comes in your name.

Gessopalena, my village, has been destroyed. The Germans have killed my sister, Bambina, who is survived by her five very young daughters. They have also wounded my old mother who has now recovered in body, but who is mortally wounded in her heart by the loss of two children in 11 days. All other members of my family are fine, and they remember you with affection and they hope to see you again one day. Here I was offered some money because of the help I gave to prisoners. Naturally, I refused it.

Your friendship is much more worthy than any money. If sometime you'll remember me you can write me at the following address: Donato De Gregorio – Via Marco Aurelio Severini n. 33 – Naples

I would have taken with pleasure some tasks behind

the enemy lines for example at Bassano del Grappa (Vicenza) or in France, if possible for you, please do something to this end and if in carrying on such tasks I shall die, please do remember my family.

I will live off my work, as always and I leave politics to those that in this moment feel doing it here.

Will I see you in Italy?

God knows! I brotherly shake your hand and I welcome (salute) in you the old and great England, land of strongly felt liberties. I wish to your illustrious step father, Marshal Montgomery, always more glory and good health and to you a rapid climbing of the ladder of military grades and everything that your just heart may wish for the coming Christmas. Dearly

De Gregorio Donato
Via Marco Aurelio Severino 33
Naples

Napoli, 5/I2/944

Carissimo Dich,

rientro solo oggi a Napoli e non so dirVi quanto piacere mi abbia fatto la Vostra lettera del 29/8 che ho trovato nel mio Ufficio.

Mi auguro che a qest'ora la vostra gamba sia perfettamente guarita e non Vi divertiate più a fermare altre palle tedesche.

Se e quando tornerete in Italia Voi sapete bene che qui vi sono due braccia fraterne,un cuore e una casa sempre aperte per Voi e per chiunque in Vostro nome venisse da me.

Gessopalena,il mio paese,fu distrutto.I Tedeschi mi uccisero

It was April 1945 before he was fit enough to rejoin the war,. By then, Monty and his Army Group had crossed the Rhine into Germany. My father joined his unit in Germany and happened to advance past Belsen a few weeks after it had been liberated.

*

At 5.30 in the morning, I hear a scratching sound on the baby monitor and walk sleepily down the corridor to find my father sitting on the side of the bed. He complains that his feet feel cold, despite the heavy eiderdown.

"I feel like a skeleton, like one of those poor people in the concentration camps," he says.

"What do you remember of the camp?" I ask him.

He doesn't say anything for some time. Then there's a small break in the clouds and a memory emerges.

"We posted photographs of the inmates and the conditions inside the camp in the nearby villages, but the Germans just shook their heads when they saw them. They didn't believe it had happened, they thought it was all Allied propaganda."

It's now daylight and he falls asleep as the *Times* lands with a smack on the gravel drive outside his window, carrying news from a world he no longer has the energy to care about.

It is too late to go back to bed so I cross the corridor into his study, and out of one of the boxes pull a copy of Monty's visitors' book that he kept in his caravan. Everyone who came to stay with him was told to leave an entry. I turn to the end.

On 3rd May 1945, there are the signatures of four Germans. General-Admiral von Friedeburg, General Kinsel, Rear Admiral Wagner and Major Friedel: the four commanders who arrived unexpectedly that day at Monty's headquarters on Luneburg Heath to discuss terms of surrender. Monty informed them that there were no terms: the surrender must be unconditional. They returned the next day and surrendered unconditionally; Monty must have told them to sign his visitors' book at the same time, as if they were his house guests. Von Friedeburg killed himself in despair shortly afterwards.

Three weeks later, on the 24th May, Churchill called on Monty.

"This record of military glories reaches its conclusion", Churchill wrote in the visitors' book. "The fame of the Army Group, like that of the Eighth Army, will long shine in history and other generations besides our own will honour these deeds and above all the character, profound strategy and untiring zeal of their commander who marched from Egypt through Tripoli, Tunis, Sicily and southern Italy and through France, Belgium, Holland and Germany to the Baltic and the Elbe without losing a battle or even a serious action."

After that entry, there are only blank pages; the "immortal march" of Monty's army had ended and the visitors stopped coming. From Berlin a few weeks later, Monty sent a copy of the visitor's book to his stepson ("To Dick Carver with all good wishes, B.L. Montgomery, Field Marshal"). He then journeyed into peacetime as a national hero, with ticker-tape parades, honorary degrees and the freedoms of distant cities that he had no intention of visiting.

As for Richard, he had given little thought to how he was going to handle the blank pages of his future. Without a war to fight, life became more complicated.

He could have chosen to take off his uniform. No one would have suggested that he hadn't more than done his duty; he had fought all through North Africa, Italy, France and Germany. He was 31 and still young enough to start a new career – perhaps in architecture, the field that he'd once hoped to study.

For someone like Richard who had only known an imperial life, Britain after the war felt diminished and disorientating. Though the Allies had won, London had the air of a defeated city. Rubble covered the streets. The government was bankrupt and

Instrument of Surrender

of

All German armed forces in HOLLAND, in

northwest Germany including all islands,

and in DENMARK.

1. The German Command agrees to the surrender of all German armed
   forces in HOLLAND, in northwest GERMANY including the FRISIAN
   ISLANDS and HELIGOLAND and all other islands, in SCHLESWIG-
   HOLSTEIN, and in DENMARK, to the C.-in-C. 21 Army Group.
   This to include all naval ships in these areas.
   These forces to lay down their arms and to surrender unconditionally.

2. All hostilities on land, on sea, or in the air by German forces
   in the above areas to cease at 0800 hrs. British Double Summer Time
   on Saturday 5 May 1945.

3. The German Command to carry out at once, and without argument or
   comment, all further orders that will be issued by the Allied
   Powers on any subject.

4. Disobedience of orders, or failure to comply with them, will be
   regarded as a breach of these surrender terms and will be dealt
   with by the Allied Powers in accordance with the accepted laws
   and usages of war.

5. This instrument of surrender is independent of, without prejudice
   to, and will be superseded by any general instrument of surrender
   imposed by or on behalf of the Allied Powers and applicable to Germany
   and the German armed forces as a whole.

6. This instrument of surrender is written in English and in German.

   The English version is the authentic text.

7. The decision of the Allied Powers will be final if any doubt or
   dispute arises as to the meaning or interpretation of the surrender
   terms.

B. L. Montgomery
Field-Marshal

5 May 1945
1830 hrs.

The surrender document, misdated May 5th 1945.
It was actually signed on May 4th

He decided to stay in the Army, with what was familiar, telling himself that he was simply continuing a career he had had before the war began, and hoping that his wartime achievements would be rewarded with promotion in peace. The army's mission was to caulk the Empire's leaky hull as best it could, and the first posting he received was to Egypt, a British colony that was rapidly becoming ungovernable.

Richard felt he needed to make up for lost time "on the marriage front". He was good-looking, well educated and carried a mild aura of reflected glory through his connection to Monty. He was also refreshingly free of the bravado and chauvinism that most army officers possessed. It wasn't long before he fell in love.

In Egypt, he met Julie O'Bryen, the daughter of a British navigation pilot on the Suez Canal, a petite, 19-year-old blonde with a large captivating smile. They dated for a year and got married in Folkestone in 1947. Richard's side was poorly represented at the wedding: his mother was dead, and his only brother John was far away in India. Monty had become Chief of the Imperial General Staff, the highest post in the British Army, inheriting the role from his old mentor Brooke. Richard assumed he would be too busy to turn up but to everyone's surprise he appeared at the church, delivered by his spotless staff car with the pennants of Field Marshal and CIGS fluttering over the headlights.

They took their honeymoon on Dartmoor. Julie stuck a series of small black and white photographs into an album, showing the two of them posing on horseback in a farmer's yard. Richard looks tall and comfortable in the saddle while Julie looks nervous, as if she is not used to being around horses. And something about the way she holds the reins suggests a person in a hurry to get on with her life.

The next page shows the interior of the cottage on the moor where they stayed. Julie took a photograph of each room; the bare-walled bedroom, the sitting room and the kitchen with an old iron range. Her handwriting is upright and careful, like a child's.

Richard and Julie had no chance to develop any kind of rhythm of married life, for straight after the honeymoon, he was posted to Kenya where the Kikuyu tribes were mounting a campaign of civil disobedience against British rule. He was put in charge of a company of sappers and ordered to build a road across the Serengeti from Nairobi to Lake Victoria to tighten the British military's control. He lived in a tented encampment near Tsavo, with a thorn fence around it to keep the lions out at night. There was only one other officer in the camp: 'Steve' Stephenson. Though Steve came from a more modest background than Richard, he played the role of the cultivated officer with greater adroitness and confidence. He too had recently got married – to a young Auxiliary Territorial Service sergeant called Audrey.

One night, as the two of them sat outside their tents listening to the hyenas tussling on top of the termite mounds in the dark, Steve asked Richard a favour.

"If anything happens to me, will you look after Audrey?"

The request caught Richard by surprise, he didn't know Steve that well and had never met Audrey. But he promised that he would; it was the decent thing to say.

Back in Egypt, Julie pasted a photograph into her album of herself standing alone outside their army quarters in Ismailia. "Married five months" says the caption. In the next photo, labelled December 1947, Richard reappears by her side dressed in a pinstripe suit. Julie's bulge is now obvious.

Richard made it back to Ismailia just in time for the birth in April. They called the son Christopher and gave him the middle name of Oswald, the name of Richard's father who had been killed at Gallipoli. Richard was thrilled – the blank pages in his life were beginning to fill in – and he returned to Kenya, able to imagine some kind of a future. One week later, as he was supervising a troop of men whitening stones to mark out the side of his new road, a Masai runner appeared with a telegram ordering him to return to Ismailia immediately.

There is a photo of Julie lying in her hospital bed with her ten-day-old Christopher beside her; she is staring intently into his barely open eyes as if she can hardly believe he exists, oblivious to the camera.

Next comes a photo of the outside of the hospital of St Vincent de Paul in Ismailia showing Julie's corner room with an ornate iron veranda. The heavy dark shutters on the windows are closed to keep out the heat. There is an ominous absence of people in the picture. At this point in the album, Richard's handwriting takes over. The next page carries the caption. "Last photos of Julie taken on Sunday April 18th," but eight small dabs of glue are all that remain on the heavy black page. The photos have been torn out.

The images resume with a picture of her grave: "Julie Aida Carver, beloved young wife of Major ROH Carver, died Ismailia 9th May 1948". She had died from undiagnosed complications caused by the childbirth.

It seems as if that is the end of the photos, but then on the next page, there's a series of photographs of Julie posing in a swimsuit on the beach in Devon, presumably taken on the honeymoon. If they had been among the other honeymoon photos they would have looked quite normal but after what's just gone before, they have an unreal quality and the sunlight seems to dance off the water a little too brightly.

Christopher's christening was delayed until after the funeral. Without his mother, Christopher is held instead in his christening gown by his grandmother, Julie's mother, and surrounded by a phalanx of stern-looking female relatives. Richard stands uncertainly off to one side, looking bereft.

Wedged into the spine on this page I found a description of Julie written by Richard shortly after she'd died.

"She had a lovely oval face and sparkling hazel eyes. A small and beautifully shaped mouth which I picture framing the word 'more' after I had kissed her... she loved me with an intensity which she admitted was almost frightening... and we motored around Dartmoor singing 'The first time I saw you' to each other. If ever I should die, she once wrote, with my last thoughts I would fly back to those wild moors hand in hand with you."

Julie's death left Richard emotionally marooned. It seemed that no relationship ever lasted. He'd lost his father at two. At eleven, a bristly army major had abruptly taken his mother away. Ten years later she had died. Then came six years of fighting which had claimed the lives of many of his colleagues. When peace returned he re-engaged his heart once more and fell immediately in love – only to lose Julie on the threshold of their new life together. The accumulated grief nearly flattened him. He became increasingly withdrawn.

During that winter in the cave, Richard had felt a strong bond with Donato the dignified Neapolitan. Here was a friendship, unexpected in its origin, which might have been able to weather all vicissitudes. After they were separated at Atessa, Donato appealed to Richard not to disappear – *you know very well that here there are two brotherly arms, a heart and a house always open to you* – but his letter appears to have gone unanswered. My father did not have the energy to keep their relationship alive.

Despite being raised by a single parent, Richard had little clue how to be one himself. Since he couldn't take Christopher back to the camp in the Serengeti, the Army sent them both home, where he handed the baby over to Julie's mother and reported for duty at the Ministry of Defence.

A year later, in June 1949, he received another telegram. Steve, his friend from the Serengeti, had died from a massive heart attack, apparently brought on by his war wounds. At his funeral, from the back of the church, he stared at the young widow, wondering what he should say to her. Beside her in the pew he could see a two-year-old boy.

But for his sense of duty, he would have walked out of the

209

church and not looked back. "Look after her," Steve had asked of him. When the service was over, he introduced himself to Audrey outside the church.

"I was a colleague of Steve's. From Kenya," he said. He told her how sorry he was to hear of Steve's death and wondered what Steve had told her. "I have a boy too. He's about the same age as yours."

"They could play together," said Audrey. "Rex would like that. He needs a friend to distract him." She didn't tell him that she was also pregnant with Steve's second child.

Audrey's family lived in a cramped terraced house near Bournemouth that backed onto salt marshes. The family kept chickens in their back yard and sold the eggs to supplement their income. Her father taught art at Bournemouth College and scraped a living as an artist. Audrey used her widow's pension to buy an abandoned fisherman's cottage on the banks of the Avon river.

The first time Richard came down to visit her, she asked him to accompany her on an expedition round the boatyards. He was startled at the sight of this pregnant woman lifting up tarpaulins and boat covers and scouring the boatsheds in search of timber and paint that she could use to renovate her cottage. But her mildly bohemian life and her small cottage reminded him of Betty's cottage on the Thames, and her spirit and energy lightened the grim ration-bound atmosphere of England. He admired the way she revelled in life despite the strain of raising two tiny children and a pain in her back which the doctors seemed unable to cure.

Sitting at his desk in Whitehall he started to write to her during his lunch hours.

After she gave birth in February 1950, Audrey asked him to be a godfather. Using his god-daughter as a excuse, his visits became more frequent. She could see that he was holding many things back and assumed it was the war that had made him like that. A lot of young men carried that slightly distant stare, as if they weren't fully participating in the present. She tried to bring him out of himself with activity. She got him to help her paint the walls; they went sailing together in her little dinghy with the old canvas sails and took their three children up onto Hengistbury Head where they picnicked among the sand dunes and chased the oystercatchers. Audrey began to fall in love.

She teased Richard about his puritan habits; she noticed the way he endlessly reused the same piece of paper, folding it over and over, rubbing out and then rewriting in pencil on the same space.

"It's as if you're still in POW camp," she said laughing.

Audrey saw no point in denial for the sake of it. She was frugal because she had no choice, she had no money, whereas Richard's austerities belonged to some kind of moral framework for he had an officer's salary and a private income. They were very different characters, like Betty and Monty had been. Over the Easter weekend of 1950 Richard asked Audrey if she would consider getting married. Audrey turned him down. She said she wasn't ready for Steve was still in her thoughts every day.

"You must understand", he wrote the next day to try to explain his behaviour, "that I have not had much experience of women. Having no sisters, my mother having died before the war and having only lived with Julie a matter of months that is probably why I failed to appreciate what your reaction would be. I did not think of how you must have a longing for security and stability after the storm you have weathered and see that is your little house. Whereas I come along and offer to uproot you even before you are in and give you that Army life again which you probably hated."

But a month later, Audrey just as abruptly changed her mind. Without a husband she knew that she would always be living on the verge of poverty. The only job she had done was to drive lorries in the blackouts and she had two children to look after. They were both still dealing with the ghosts of previous marriages and did not know each other well, but they would make it work somehow. Richard was delighted.

211

Richard and Audrey at their wedding

When Richard informed his stepfather that he was getting remarried, Monty replied he didn't see the point. Like Richard, Monty was struggling to find his feet in the post-war world. His brusqueness and lack of tact, endurable in war, could no longer be overlooked. His tenure as Chief of the Imperial General Staff was not a success and after just two years he was shuffled to the continent to be commander-in-chief for the Western European Union, a forerunner of NATO.

"I was summoned to Monty's office yesterday," Richard wrote to Audrey in June. "He had our engagement notice in front of him and suggested that I should put in his name if I was going to say 'son of etc'. Also he said that I must say you are a widow 'to protect you', otherwise people will think you are divorced!"

They were married on September 25th 1950. Monty turned up, walking down the aisle with Audrey's parents, the presence of the Field Marshal making front-page news in the *Christchurch Times*.

*

One day during that summer, Richard got a phone call from Jim Gill saying he was in town.

"On Wednesday I gave lunch to Jim Gill and his wife who are here on a short visit from South Africa," he wrote to Audrey. "I saw him last on Dec 1st 1943 when we parted behind the German lines. He looked a bit fatter than at that time, but otherwise much the same. He had left his wife in England and gone off to Italy for a week to re-visit the old haunts.

"He found the cave and Donato's mother was at the cottage, but Donato himself had disappeared rather mysteriously and no-one professed to know where he was. Of course, he had great difficulty getting to these places and said he was astonished at the distances we had walked…"

The Dean too had been back to Italy and was eager to tell Richard about how he had visited some of the places that he and Richard had walked through.

"I had dinner with 'The Dean' and his sister last night. They were most enthusiastic about their Italian trip and gave me the address of a convent hostel above Florence where they stayed, which sounded very good. They went by car and took a young English priest with them to act as guide and interpret. It must have been a very funny party. The Dean offered to give us a coffee percolator, similar to his own, as a wedding present."

Richard suggested to Audrey that they go to Italy for their honeymoon. They went to Florence, Pisa, Portofino, Orta, Maggiore and Baveno but they do not seem to have gone anywhere with any connection to his time in the war. With his compass and his makeshift map he had walked unscathed through some of the most well known parts of Italy. But in the photograph album that remains of their honeymoon, the only pictures of any Italians are the staff of the Hotel Sempione in Baveno. The de Gregorio family are nowhere to be seen.

Having given Richard his account of their adventures, the Dean suggested that Richard write up his own version before he forgot. Richard took out the miniscule green notebook that he'd carried with him on the run and copied his account into a school exercise book with a wine red cover. At the entry for 24th November 1943 – the day that the German patrol came looking for them in the cave – he stuck in a studio photo of Donato with a gauzy background of Tuscan hills behind. Donato's face with its small neat beard is turned slightly away, but his eyes look straight at the camera.

Two years later, in 1952, the army ordered Richard back to Ismailia for a second tour of duty. It was nearly a year before the situation in Egypt was considered safe enough for Audrey and the children to join him. By then she had given birth to twins. "I know life will be full and happy with our children my darling," Audrey wrote on 11th February 1953 "and there will be no time to grieve but always my love for you will underline the absence of your physical presence and I shall not feel complete until we are together again."

Richard was also desperate for them to be reunited and wrote back frequently, sometimes three or four times in a week. Eventually she arrived after a gruelling journey by sea with five children. It cannot have been easy for either of them living in the camp where he and Julie had met and lived together. Richard barely mentioned Julie to the family, which only increased the presence of her ghost. He found it easier to withdraw his memories into some private space, inaccessible to anyone else. Audrey did the opposite, bringing Steve up in conversation as much as possible as she tried to find a way to entwine the memory of him into her new life. She wore the wedding ring Steve had given her just below Richard's ring, so that I grew up assuming that all widows wore two rings of different gold.

*

In July 1958, the Ministry of Defence told Richard that they had an important mission for him. The news at first came as a shock: the posting was on Christmas Island in the Pacific Ocean where Britain was testing its first generation of nuclear bombs. Knowing his hunger for promotion, they stroked his ego: it's a good career move; you'll be the senior army officer on the island, in charge of protecting the nuclear scientists. They played on his patriotism: this is the secret weapon that will keep Britain at the centre of world affairs and a force to be reckoned with, we need men like you to help secure our place at the top table, they said.

The posting would be for two years and unaccompanied. We're not set up for wives or families, they told him bluntly.

The newspapers were full of descriptions of this heroic new frontier. "H Bomb puts Britain on level terms." "Britain's emergence as top-ranking power." The breathless articles described how each bomb was suspended below four helium balloons and detonated in the air with scientific accuracy. Clean, technological and devastating, the nuclear bomb is a fitting symbol for the Age of the Common Man, said the editorials.

In time, Richard would learn that Britain was trying to become a nuclear superpower on the cheap. The soldiers on the island had been close to mutinying because of their poor diet and jerry-built accommodation, that the "miracle bombs" were crude devices and the wondrous technological balloons only old barrage balloons left over from the war.

Audrey longed for him to forsake his duty and stay with his family but knew that it was not within his nature and so she did not ask. They spent their final night together at Carol Mather's parents' large house overlooking Wimbledon Common. In the morning, Audrey drove him down to Heathrow.

> *As the plane taxied down the runway, Audrey waved a yellow umbrella from the spectators' enclosure. Audrey very good about it right up to the end, a very gallant woman.*

The BOAC flight went first to New York, then stopped briefly to refuel in a San Francisco shrouded in mist, before finally heading out over the Pacific to Honolulu. The next morning, he caught an RAF Hastings plane on to Christmas Island. The isolation of the atoll felt immediately familiar.

"I find I am living in the Task Force Command mess," he wrote on his first evening with evident satisfaction. "A delightful place looking straight out to sea."

There were ten officers in the Task Force Command mess. Each night they would dress for dinner and gather for a chota-peg on the mess balcony to stare out over the unplumbed sea. The distances were mesmerizing; the closest continent was 5,000 miles in any direction. The old hands pointed out that they were balancing on a spike of coral one mile high.

"When the early tests happened, everyone was afraid that the blast waves might snap the coral's slender stem, sending the island and everyone on it plunging to the bottom."

They all laughed together at the absurdity of the idea. And yet it was apt. They had all lived through the war and knew that nothing lasted; life was a slender stem which could be swiftly severed. But these were emotions which they could not discuss with each other. Richard found the indirectness of their interaction comforting. Here on this atoll his relationships with others could be kept at an undemanding level; no one challenged his equilibrium.

The month before he arrived, there'd been three nuclear tests on the island – more than ever before – and it seemed like the

**Richard "talking to Corporal Simpkins in the Corporals' Club" –
during the visit by Duke of Edinburgh to Christmas Island
in April 1959**

programme was accelerating, but it wasn't. Eisenhower and the
Russians had agreed to a moratorium on nuclear testing and England had quickly followed suit. Richard asked whether he should
come home, but the Ministry said that he should continue with his
mission as normal. He was to supervise the building of the airfield,
the roads and the flying-boat port. Britain had every intention of
resuming the tests once the moratorium was lifted, the MOD told
him.

In fact, the moratorium offered a convenient way to close the
program without the embarrassment of pleading penury, and soon
the scientists began to leave, and the stream of MPs from London
and American admirals from Okinawa dried up. Before long, the
only visitors were the black frigate birds and the storm petrels that
floated in on the ocean currents, resting for a few days on this dot
in the undulating blanket of endless sea. The only indication that

there had ever been nuclear tests were the bodies of the fish and birds which continued to wash up on the beaches for several weeks afterwards, killed by the shock waves from the blast.

Richard moved away from the officers' mess to camp on the coral:

I have moved my tent to the edge of the sea and now hear the surf continuously and can see the broad Pacific in all lights; sunset, moonlight and sunrise. At high tide the sea comes to within 10 yards of my tent and about six feet below the level of it down a steep little bank of broken coral. It is really very lovely and at night wonderfully peaceful. I am sending some shells home by a ship."

He had returned to the cave. He spent his days striding over the hard coral in long khaki shorts; his skin turning red, then brown then black in the blinding sun. If he wondered to what purpose his new asphalt runway and the freshly painted concrete accommodation blocks would be put, he did not confide such doubts in his diaries. He was content. At weekends, he snorkelled slowly around the reefs and lagoons staring at the tropical fish, and bobbed on the swell in fishing boats catching wahoo and tuna.

At home, Audrey struggled to cope with the demands of five children under the age of 12. She was exhausted by the constant rounds of winter flus, coughs, measles, adenoids and accidents but tried hard to keep her letters sounding upbeat.

The family's only proof that Richard was alive were letters and the occasional coconut, a fruit almost unknown in 1950s England outside the coconut shies of travelling fairs. Each one had the name of a child and our address painted in white road-marking paint around the coconut's tummy with two rows of brightly coloured stamps glued firmly on the hairy head. When the postman pulled one out of his tattered postbag with a flourish, it'd be greeted with squeals of delight and thrown from one child to the next, held and admired. There was intense discussion about

Audrey and the six children – and Sally, the dog

the journey it had taken; the twins imagined the coconuts sitting on the deck of a dhow as it made its way through the shark-infested waters of the Pacific.

Richard returned home in November 1959, after fourteen months away. In his absence the family had been forced to adjust to being without a father, and he made little attempt to reassert his authority. He maintained the façade of the affable, courteous army officer who enjoyed talking politics and religion, but behind it, Richard the person was becoming increasingly hard to find. He had returned from Christmas Island, only to absent himself in other ways.

I was born one year later. The Sixties washed over us all, turning my older brothers and sisters from curly-headed eight year olds into surly, hormonal teenagers and the Beatles. They ignored their father's orders to be home by midnight. Crashed motorbikes and flunked exams. Richard did not understand the social revolution that was going on and saw their rebellion only as further evidence of his own irrelevancy.

Christmas Island did not deliver the hoped for promotion. He felt he had failed to produce a career of any substance, especially when measured by the yardstick of his stepfather. Monty, the one person who might have intervened on his behalf, was of no use. He had retired from public life a disappointed man and lived alone at Isington Mill, absorbed by his own past.

One day in 1966 Richard found himself running the welfare and administration records at the Royal Engineers Records Office outside Brighton. He was no longer in charge of any soldiers, just their paper records. He decided to resign. After thirty years in the army, he had no idea what to do next. He thought vaguely of becoming a vicar but Audrey, who had no intention of becoming a vicar's wife, adamantly refused. In October, he interviewed with Clark's Shoes. In December, he discussed the possibility of joining Unilever. In January he decided to become a teacher. He was offered a post teaching physics and maths at Marlborough public school and given one week's training.

In the teachers' common room, he struggled to relate to the young socialist teachers who argued over whether boarding schools in the Soviet Union were preferable to the English public school system. The Empire was considered an embarrassment and no one seemed to believe any longer in God. The Second World War – the defining experience of his life – was now just part of the curriculum. The school assumed that as a military man he would be a disciplinarian, but it wasn't in Richard's nature to be harsh. He had been through too much confinement to have any interest in inflicting punishment on others. He stuck it out for six years, first at Marlborough, then Radley, and finally asked the Army to take him back. They gave him a retired officer's job editing training manuals in Chatham, Kent. It was 1972. As far as the world was concerned he was just another mild-mannered middle-aged civil servant.

One night during the Easter holidays that year, my mother's appendix ruptured. By now I was the only child still living at home.

"Don't worry, I'll be fine," she said, waving weakly at my father and me as she was wheeled past us to the waiting ambulance. I was scared and wondered if I was going to see her again. Throughout my life, my mother had been the one constant, steady force of happiness for me. My father and I stood in the doorway and watched the blue lights of the ambulance recede into the rainy night. I was 11 years old and had never before been on my own with my father. Up to this moment, he had been little more than an ornamentation in my upbringing. He would come home in the evenings from the office and disappear into his study. Weekends he would spend in his potting shed or at church. Each Saturday morning when I was not at boarding school, he would present my pocket money to me (one pre-decimalisation penny for every year of my age) with a little pat on the head.

His potting-shed was one of the few places I felt his presence. I happily volunteered to help him "do jobs" to be near him; it was the one time I felt permitted to be in his world. He had no idea, I think, how much I loved being in there with him. Sometimes, when I had held a piece of wood that he was nailing or sawing or varnishing, he would thank me by a brief hug around my shoulders. I longed to be close to him, but outside the potting shed I had no idea how to do it.

I noticed how little he ever talked about himself, to the point of self-denial. I assumed that all fathers were as removed as he was.

Where the hell have you been?

In the bigger context of my father's life, Monty's question was curiously apt. Having lost so much, my father had anaesthetized himself against any further pain by engaging in our lives only intermittently. His unconscious tendency was to move towards the edges, away from the focus of attention. My mother had tried to keep him connected to the family, but she had always had the army pulling him in the opposite direction.

My mother was given an emergency operation that night. When she eventually emerged from hospital, she suggested that we go to Italy on holiday to recuperate. It was during that trip that we made the unexpected detour to Fontanellato, and Richard Carver began to come into focus.

17.

In 1979 MY father finally retired completely, and my parents bought the house by the sea. Seven years later, my mother contracted cancer and died. They had been together for thirty-five years and everyone assumed – his children, his friends – that without my mother my father would be lost, too unworldly to be able to handle life on his own. He had never opened a recipe book and had no idea how to operate the washing machine. But we were all too focused on the practicalities, which showed how little any of us really knew him.

Imagining that he must be lonely I came down from London where I was then living to see him as often as possible. He loved to walk and so we would stride across the fields to the Gun Inn that overlooked the Solent, or push our way through thick bracken to some pub hidden within the green darkness of the New Forest.

I watched a slow metamorphosis come over him. He started to become more accessible. And at the same time he subconsciously began to dismantle his physical appearance. A tie and jacket had always been a part of the artifice of the proper Englishman that held him in place – like going every Sunday to church and reading *The Times* at breakfast. He had worn a tie everyday in the week and even at weekends he had felt the need to wear a cravat. But now I noticed he wore his shirts unbuttoned at the collar.

He began to give glimpses of a life I'd never seen before.

He laughed as he told me how he'd travelled by boat a thousand miles up the Amazon river at the age of nine, taken by an aunt desperate for a break from a claustrophobic marriage. And he laughed again as he recounted coming down one morning to breakfast in an Austrian guesthouse during a walking holiday in the 1930s to find that the Anschluss had taken place in the night and there were German soldiers everywhere.

Bit by bit he re-emerged. With my mother gone, he had no one left to hide behind. He found himself the centre of his children's attention for the first time. That vivid flash of understanding that I'd had as an 11-year-old looking up at him, as I lay in the ditch beside Fontanellato, came back to me. For forty years he had been missing in action, telling himself that he was irrelevant, with extraordinary stories bottled inside him.

When he turned eighty, I took my father up to London to attend the opening of a new "Monty Exhibit" at the Imperial War Museum. Monty had been dead eighteen years, consigned to history books. We joined a queue of elderly Eighth Army veterans and London schoolchildren outside the Museum, my father reluctant as ever to pull rank of any kind. He was excited by our "little jaunt together" as he called it.

Before long, a young man in a blazer and tie bustled over and introduced himself as the chief curator.

"I recognised you from photos in the books about Monty," he said to my father who seemed flattered. "There is a section about Monty's personal life with one or two photos of your family in the exhibition."

We walked slowly around the memorabilia, my father leaning

on my arm. Dozens of images of Monty stared out at us from the walls. I had discovered from our pub walks that his relationship with Monty was more complicated than it'd seemed. He showed me the anguished letter that Monty wrote to my father the day of Betty's death – "I feel desperately lonely and sad. I suppose in time I shall get over it, but at present it seems that I never shall" – and it made me realise how much the two of them had been united in their grief for the same woman.

In time I was to come across other letters from Monty expressing concern about Richard's safety in the war. Monty's overbearing personality had left no room for Richard's more fragile character to grow. But now the man who had dominated my father's life was locked safely inside a row of glass cabinets. My father seemed both relieved, and at the same time curiously protective of him and his war record.

"Monty was always criticised for being too cautious as a general, even by Churchill," my father mused as we studied the many publicity shots that Monty had so carefully orchestrated. "But he had good reason to be cautious: he hated wasting men's lives unnecessarily."

Our first sight of Monty's two caravans was from the floor above where an old First World War plane had been suspended from the roof.

"We have left them exactly as they were in his garden at the Mill, with the D Day caravan on the left and the desert one on the right," the curator commentated cheerfully as we leant over the railing.

I felt chill memories of Sunday exeats from Dumpton and the dread of being taken back to school by my parents in time for evensong. Surrounded by large howitzers and tanks, the caravans looked much less grand than I remembered.

We waited our turn outside. There was room for only a couple of people at a time in each caravan. Inside, I could see two American veterans were leaning over Monty's desk and scrutinising the chinagraph battle lines on the map.

"Fascinating," I heard one say to his colleague. "Take a look at this. You can see from these markings that Monty was planning to advance two entire divisions by sea."

"Why on earth would he have done that?" said the other.

"Perhaps he had a plan to outflank Rommel with an amphibious landing."

"Monty was a more cunning general than I've given him credit for."

Over their shoulder, I could see the faint outlines of my impulsive ten year old scribbles into the Mediterranean. As we were leaving the museum I told my father the story of what I had done and he gave a deep snorting laugh.

*

One morning in December 1995, a package arrived for my father in the post. I placed it beside him on the breakfast table. He put down his copy of the *Times* and pulled out the tiny mother of pearl penknife which he always carried and slit open the crumpled brown paper wrapping.

Inside was a videocassette and a card from an address in Switzerland. In formal but somewhat halting English, the writer explained that he had located my father's address through the British embassy in Geneva and wished my father a rapid return to health. It was signed by an Antonio Lannutti.

"I wasn't aware I had been ill," my father said, blinking his eyebrows up and down at me in amusement.

He picked up the video. It was void of all markings. By the way he looked at it, turning it over slowly in his large hands, I could tell that he had no idea what its purpose was so I spent the morning buying a video recorder at the electrical store in the village, then lying on my stomach on his old Amman rugs trying to make the brightly coloured wires of the appliance fit the sockets of his ancient television.

"It will allow you to record programmes on TV," I said to help him to justify what he clearly thought was a large and superfluous expense.

"Oh good," he said gamely, "you must show me how I do that," though we both knew that he would never show enough interest to learn. By lunchtime I had managed to make it work. We sat in the curtained gloom of an English afternoon, the December rain tapping at the windows, and I pressed play. The video opened with a slight jerk, a susurration in the darkness. Then an old lady, dressed in a widow's black and Italian-looking, appeared. She sat staring into the camera, her eyes fogged by cataracts, saying nothing. She seemed toothless and of enormous age.

"This lady sitting here is the lady who cooked all your meals when you used to go up to the house. This is Maria, the mother of the boy Alfonso," said an unseen voice in English with a thick Italian accent. It meant nothing to me then.

The film jumped to a collapsed farmhouse and a track, steep and chalky, falling down into the underwater shadows of a wood in summer. Three figures were walking downhill, one of them going partly sideways to preventing himself from stumbling on the loose chalk. With their jerseys tied around their waist, they looked as if they were on a day hike. The film could have been made anytime in the last fifty years. One of the men, balding, with a warm friendly smile, introduced himself as Antonio Lannutti, the author of the letter. He explained that he was a relative of the De Gregorio family.

"Mr Carver," he said, "this is the track the Germans were going down on the morning that they stole the pig."

I looked over at my father for an explanation. He was leaning forward in his chair studying the TV screen closely. From nowhere a video had appeared of a memory more than fifty years old. One of the other men, slightly older than Antonio, set off half walking, half running down the track, followed by the camera. Waving vigorously at the thick canopy of sycamore and oak saplings beside the track, he halted at a bend while the camera continued moving up and down as the camera operator caught his breath.

The man told the cameraman to aim at the undergrowth and a figure swam into focus from the shadows – it was a boy, no more than 17 or 18, who was attempting to burrow his body under the brambles. The man lunged off the track and grabbed the boy's leg, pulling him out into the sunlight.

The man talked rapidly in Italian as the balding Antonio explained what was going on.

"This is Alfonso who found you that day… they were looking for a place to ambush the Germans and to kill them so that they could get their pig."

"And this," he said, pointing to the youth lying awkwardly in the brambles, "is my son, Gino. He is lying in the exact spot where Alfonso tripped over you and Jim. You were shaking with fear."

Alfonso grinned proudly at the camera while Gino, his son, stood up, looking a little sheepish.

"'Who are you?' I said to you that day. And Jim and you replied, 'we are English prisoners of war.' Mr Carver, do you remember?"

My father had sunk back in his chair, verging on tears. For fifty years, this family in Italy had held tightly to the memory of Richard and what had happened in the war. He mattered to them, and this was their appeal to him for contact. They were determined not to let this one small grain of memory dissolve in the vast sea of the war.

I tried to piece together what I knew. This man, now standing in his shirtsleeves with his thick sunburnt farmer's arms crossed across his chest, was the 14-year-old Alfonso who first found Jim and Richard in the bushes. But it was only much later that I came to realise that Maria, the blind woman at the beginning, was the person who had negotiated with the German commander for the pig's release.

The video went to black once more and then a moment later,

Alfonso reappeared, scrambling up what looked like a small rock face. He sat aside a rock and pointed inside a large hole..

"This is where you and Jim lived for those weeks," said Antonio. "It must have been very cold for you in there, I think."

It was the entrance to the cave. I stared into the black mouth, trying to place my father there, imagining him drying his socks on the bushes outside that Antonio was now absently swishing with a birch. Alfonso pointed to the top of the crag.

"And this is where the Germans stood that day," Antonio translated, trying to keep up with Alfonso's excited commentary, "and they urged you and Jim to surrender. You see it was very close to where you were. You were almost touching them."

Until that afternoon this strange story of the family of three brothers in the farmhouse with the pig and the cave in the woods had always had the quality of a family fairytale, which happened too long ago to be able to be fully verified. But that day the worlds of myth and the everyday fused together. Here was the family that my father had told me about. Somewhere in the Apennines, these places and these people actually existed.

The final images on the film were of the family cemetery – the headstones of the de Gregorio parents and below them their three sons: Giovanni, Antonio and Donato. Antonio's had the date of November 27th 1943, the day he died from his injuries in the British bombing raid. The camera pans to Donato's. The photo on his headstone is the same as the one in my father's diary. I grab the remote and freeze the image. The date on his headstone says 1976. So all during the sixties – when my father thought he was dead – he was actually alive and living in Italy.

I pointed out the date to my father.

"He was probably living in Naples the day that we drove through on our holiday in 1972," I said.

"Huh, I thought he'd died much earlier than that," was all he said.

Alfonso peered into the camera, as if hoping to find my

father somewhere inside its cogs and lens. "I hope you enjoyed all these little bits of wartime from Italy, Mr Carver, " said Antonio. Then the image on the screen went black and my father reached for a pen and wrote carefully on the video's spine: "*The old farm at Gessopalena and the cave where I hid behind German lines in Italy in Dec '43. Sent me by a Signor Lanotti [sic] Dec '95.*"

He sucked in his breath and held it for a second then sank back into his chair. I watched him, waiting for him to speak. I could see he was struggling to decide what to say. He was clearly moved, but now that it was over he seemed unsurprised, as if it was what he had expected all along.

"Would you like some more tea?" he asked.

*

My father dutifully wrote to Antonio Lannutti in Geneva, thanking him for the gift. Mr Lannutti wrote back immediately, relieved and delighted that it had reached its destination. The following year Mr Lannutti turned up on my father's doorstep. He explained that he and his wife, who turned out to be from Essex, were on a motoring holiday in England, visiting her relatives. My father invited them to lunch.

After that, the Lannuttis called on my father every summer for several years. He put them on his Christmas card list and wrote back whenever they wrote to him. They invited him to visit Gessopalena and Alfonso, who was still living in Gessopalena, but he didn't take them up. I do not know why. Perhaps it was because there was no Donato any more, or perhaps, by entertaining the Lannuttis for lunch, he felt he had closed the loop.

Eventually the visits by the Lannuttis dried up and my father stopped writing Christmas cards. In 2003 he made one final trip to Italy, to Fontanellato for the sixtieth anniversary of the escape. By then he was 89 and he found the trip exhausting. Nine "old contemptibles" were all that were left out of a camp of six hundred. In the exercise yard at the back, they cut a ribbon at midday as a bugler played and walked out in a ragged line, a red triangle of cloth pinned to their jackets in memory of the POW flashes they'd had to wear on their backs. A farmer told Richard how he remembered being sent as a boy with his sister to give baskets of bread and grapes to the prisoners in the overgrown ditch.

The video however stayed on top of his television, its little white label greying in the English light. It took on the same ornamental status as Aunt Bulley's china: he showed no interest in it yet he didn't throw it away. In time, I came to understand that my father wore all his experiences lightly. He was not someone who had much interest in returning to the past and dwelling on it. He lived in the present – it was one of his appealing qualities that he still showed such a strong interest in the world around him, even in his late eighties. Yet for myself I found that I needed to know more. Every so often in America, I fretted that Alfonso might soon die, and then the last direct connection to what had happened would be lost for ever.

18.

By May 2007 my father is close to dying. He is 93. I have spent the last twelve months shuttling back and forth across the Atlantic from my home in Washington, trying to have as much time as possible in his presence.

I realise that I have been doing much the same for the last two decades; returning at the end of each trip I made into some foreign continent to the house by the sea to sit in the garden with him.

It's 2am. I enter his bedroom and he opens his eyes, studying me from inside the weak circle of light emitted by his bedside lamp.

"Where have you been?" he asks.

"Nowhere."

"I'm not dead yet you know," he says managing a smile before falling back into sleep.

I enjoy my vigils by his bed; I like the intimacy that darkness brings, the way that the hours stretch out after midnight, punctuated only by an occasional car passing by on the road outside.

"I am stuck," he mutters in his sleep, "I can't see him…

Richard Carver in his last years

I wish this mist would lift."

He twitches as if he's trying to dodge something, though his old bones won't allow him to move very far. He lives in a form of twilight with memories rising to the surface of his mind like twigs in a muddy river water stirred up by a storm.

The days exhaust him. He seldom moves outside the house now. The carers can no longer cope with him and his house; getting him up from a chair takes twenty minutes and two people. Mice run freely through the kitchen and his bedroom. Large chunks of plaster, their cracks covered uselessly by sellotape, are breaking off like ice floes and falling on the furniture. His world has been reduced to two rooms: his bedroom and the dining room where he sits all day. The other rooms of the house feel cold and neglected. Despite the tartan rug over his knees and the gas fire on full he complains of feeling cold.

It is time for him to leave. The pages of his W.H. Smiths calendar which until last summer were full of lunches, army reunions, house groups, church events and lectures, are now blank white spaces. His friends are either dead or too ill themselves to visit.

There is a nursing home near my sister's farm in southern Scotland which has agreed to take him. It was once the main pub in my sister's village; I remember seeing the fishermen, tanked up with Tartan beer, surging out the door. Ghostly figures now sit in the room that used to be the public bar without speaking all day.

In his little bedroom my sisters have hung the oar he won at Cambridge and a painting of Quetta done by Betty in 1936 to help him feel at home. He lasts the remainder of the spring there, eating bananas with a fork and watching the sheep moving slowly across the damp hills. Then in July, he is taken to the local hospital suffering from pneumonia.

On the last day that I see my father, he is propped up in his hospital bed, drinking tea through a straw. We sit together in a companionable silence, looking out at the fat cow-soaked hills of Dumfries. He slips noiselessly in and out of sleep, clutching his tea. His face is as still as a death mask when he's sleeping, as if he is halfway to death already. I hold his bony hand and can just make out his flickering pulse. He wakes confused as if he had been away for a long time, though it was only a few seconds. Then his eyes find me.

"Ah Tom," he says softly to himself. I smile, hoping this might be the start of a conversation, but he drifts off once more.

I watch the nurses help the old lady drink her tea in the next door bed. She pecks at it like a bird.

"Where's Jude?" my father says suddenly. "He'll cheer me up." I'm thrilled that he remembers my son's name; wherever he's going I hope he will carry some memory of his seven-year-old grandson with him.

Bored by looking at his books, Jude has wandered out into

234

the corridor where he's playing a game with his two year old sister, letting her waddle down towards the nurses' station before chasing after her. Each time he catches her, she gurgles with delight.

Hearing his name called, he returns and stands a little anxiously at the foot of my father's bed reluctant to go any closer, as if death is infectious. I remember being summoned to say goodbye to Monty when he was dying and my father telling me to stand at the end of his bed so that Monty could see me. I was surprised how small his bedroom was. I did not think of him as my grandfather; there seemed to be so little that was paternal in him; he was just Monty.

"What are you going to do when you grow up?" Monty had asked me once last time, that famous brisk voice now horse and frayed.

"Be a soldier sir," I'd said and felt my father exhale beside me, relieved that I hadn't said anything inappropriate. I was 15 by then so could easily have done so. Monty nodded – it was what he was expecting to hear.

"What are you going to do with your life?" is what my father asks of Jude. It is a gentler, open-ended question. I look at my son and wonder what will come out.

"Be a soldier," he says unexpectedly. Dad blinks at him but says nothing. He seems rather surprised.

EPILOGUE

My father died on July 24th 2007. He left behind many mysteries – not least the fate of the de Gregorios. I felt a debt of gratitude needed to be repaid which my father, normally so scrupulous, had either overlooked or failed to understand. For a year it gnawed at me, until, as much for myself as for my father, I started to investigate whether there were any de Gregorios still alive. I discovered that only Alfonso remained – the boy whose pig was stolen by the Germans.

With the help of Antonio Lannutti and his British wife Barbara, the couple who had sent the video, I arranged to visit Alfonso in August with my wife and children. From Rome airport, we drove due east. Within a couple of hours, we were in a land of deep shadows and giant upheavals of rock and forest.

"It is a very upset landscape," Antonio had warned on the phone.

Small towns clung to the escarpments as if they had been blown against the rockface like pieces of litter. I thought of Jim and Richard scrambling down these slopes in the darkness, terrified of stumbling into some hidden German trench. Even in the heat of a July day, the air felt cool.

Early the next morning, Antonio and Barbara came to meet us at our hotel. Antonio was now completely bald but otherwise looked exactly the same as he had done on the video 15 years earlier. Barbara, his wife, still carried the traces of an English upbringing in her voice.

We set off in two cars, crossed the Sangro and skirted around the village of Roccascalegna which the Germans had occupied as their headquarters. Soon we were traveling through small woods and uneven fields on a road that looked like it had been recently created.

"This is the road to Gessopalena where the Germans were pushing the pig down that morning," said Antonio. "For a long time it was just a track, exactly as it used to be when your father was here, but two months ago they tarmaced it."

As the road crossed a small stream at the bottom of the valley, a man stepped out of the shade of an oak tree. It was Alfonso. He had wiry sandy hair and a weathered face and still had the look of a young boy. It was easy to see in his hopeful smile the 14-year-old so eager that day to do something brave to impress his mother. He carried a long handled machete over one shoulder and wore blue shorts and thick boots with short socks. He looked doubtfully at my children in their flip flops and tee-shirts, then hugged each of them in turn.

"I wish your father was here to see this," he said with Antonio translating. His Italian had a thick Abruzzo burr.

After a swig of water, Alfonso led us into the wood to find the cave. He started confidently at first, using his machete to clear a straight line through the brambles. After 15 minutes he paused, looked around then moved off on a new bearing. Then he stopped again.

"No wonder the Germans couldn't find it," said Jude.

"Don't worry," said Antonio gallantly holding back a branch

The author, with Antonio Lannutti, and Alfonso, the '14-year-old boy' who found Richard in the bushes in 1943

for us to pass, "Alfonso grew up in these woods, he knows exactly where it is."

After forty minutes of circling around, there was still no sign of any cave. We broke into smaller groups and fanned out in different directions until eventually Alfonso called out that he had found it and we clambered up to where he was standing.

The place fitted my father's description. Several huge boulders, heaped on top of each other, a slit between the lowest two. In

238

my father's sketches you could clearly see him and Jim being able to stand in the entrance but now the gap was less than three feet. A large amount of earth and rubble had filled in the hole raising the floor of the cave.

"There was a landslide in this area some years ago," said Alfonso. "Before that, you used to be able to see the reeds from the stream that your father and Jim had used as bedding. They were still lying on the floor of the cave."

I was not sure what I hoped to find – some evidence perhaps of his presence. I noticed a rock sticking up through the landslipped earth whose contours looked softer than the others – maybe that was the one my father used as a pillow. I tried to imagine them outside, leaning back against the boulders, my father trying hard to engage the taciturn Jim in conversation as they dried their clothes on the bushes.

On the way back, we reached the road almost immediately. It turned out the cave was only a hundred yards from where we had started. We walked up the track to the ruins of the farmhouse. The air was full of the smell of wild sage and lavender.

Alfonso described how they had lived in three rooms with their animals stabled below so that their heat warmed the house. The roof had collapsed and wild roses now curled around the fallen roof beams and broken walls where Jim and Richard had sat and listened to Donato's stories about Naples.

We drove back to Alfonso's apartment for lunch. Part of the village was completely abandoned. Alfonso explained that this was the old village of Gessopalena, where no one had lived since the war ended. "The Germans blew up everything when they left, leaving it like this," he said. The wind whispered over the cobbles, pushing around eddies of dust and litter.

We found Alfonso's wife Maria in the garage of their apartment. She was short with vivid brown eyes and a warm smile. She wore a plastic apron over her large chest, and was laying out strips of homemade pasta on top of her freezer. She showed us how to make *spaghetti alla chitarra* by pushing the pasta over several thin wires which cut the pasta into long thin strips.

"In the old days, they used the strings of a guitar, hence the name *chitarra*."

Then she led us upstairs to the dining room where the air conditioning was fighting a losing battle against the kitchen stove. Our children overwhelmed the small rooms. Exhausted by the heat and the expedition to the cave, Felix the eldest asked if he can lie down on their bed, while Maya and Jude collapsed onto their couch. Two year old Poppy discovered their bidet and washed her fat little feet with squeals of delight. I asked Maria whether they had children and she wiped her hands on her apron anxiously.

"God did not will it," Alfonso said.

They had first met when they were still at school during the war, probably about the time that Alfonso had stumbled across my father. They fell in love but their parents did not approve of their relationship as they had not arranged it, and did their best to keep them apart. Maria was sent to Canada to live with a distant cousin whilst Alfonso stayed in Gessopalena. He would write, promising to come to Canada but it was a long time before he summoned up the courage to defy his mother. He finally joined Maria in Montreal in the 1970s.

"But by then we were too old to conceive," she said simply.

They lived there for eleven years, Alfonso working as a foreman in warehouses, until eventually they returned to Gessopalena to look after the parents who had sought to keep them apart.

Alfonso took off his shirt and sat down at the table in his trousers and his white *canottiere* singlet as Maria started to bring in the food. The room had few ornaments except for a reproduction oil painting of a night-time scene at a port and a huge glass candelabra above the table. Before leaving America, I had made a photograph album of pictures of my father, my family, his sketches of the cave from his journal and his photograph of Donato. Alfonso smiled, and remembered Donato singing "*O Sole Mio*" in the kitch-

The old farmhouse at Gessopalena

en when Jim and my father came in for supper, just as my father described it.

"Donato became very fond of your father. They were good friends," he said.

I imagined Richard joining in, hesitantly at first, held back by his reserve and his lack of confidence in his Italian but then, urged on by Donato, singing with greater and greater gusto. It was an image of great happiness. I realised how much the family had grown to love my father. The efforts that they made to stay in touch – the letters from Donato, the video that they made, Antonio's visits to England to have lunch with him – were enormous. It should have been the other way around. I had come here, as much to try to find my father as to represent him: this man who had seemed so straightforward, but who had receded out of reach each time I tried to touch him.

The limoncello came out and Poppy started to motor in and out of the kitchen helping herself to Maria's sweetcakes. The moment had come to say something.

I stood up and raised my glass to drink a toast.

"Thank you," I said solemnly, "for saving my father's life. I wish that he was here to thank you himself."

Alfonso got unsteadily to his feet in return. Standing in his white singlet, he raised his glass too.

"If your father had not been so tall and if his feet had not stuck out of the bush, I would not have tripped over them," Alfonso said, gripping the back of his chair to steady himself. "Let's go for a drive – there is something I want to show you."

We drove out of Gessopalena away from Roccascalegna. After twenty minutes of sharp twists and turns through a pine forest, we turned off down a track. The sign under an old olive tree said Sant'Agata. At the end stood a broken farmhouse much like the others that lay strewn across the landscape, with bindweed curling up the walls and wild grasses billowing in the wind between the stones. It was a quiet calm place. Beyond the farmhouse the land dropped away in a steep slope and facing us across a great void of air was the huge flank of the Majella ridge.

On a small stone memorial in front of the house was a date: "21st January 1944". There then followed a list of 43 names, many of whom appeared to be women from the same few families: Luzio, Gonna, Cionne.

"A few days before this date," explained Alfonso, "someone killed four Germans who had stolen a cow. The Germans operated a system of decimation like the Romans: 10 civilians executed for every one of their soldiers. For some reason they decided on this remote farmhouse which was packed with refugees. They banged on the door and demanded to be let in. When the terrified occupants refused, blockading the door, the Germans took it to be an admission of guilt.

"The officer ordered his soldiers to climb up onto the roof and pour petrol down the chimney. As the farmhouse burned, the soldiers stood in the fields listening to the screams coming from inside. One child survived. She was eight years old, and crouched in the corner as her family died. She is still alive today and lives nearby, but luckily her mind has forgotten the experience."

"If we had killed the German soldiers that day," said Alfonso, "instead of rescuing your father and Jim, this is what would have happened to all of us. We would not be here now. It wasn't us who saved his life – it was he who saved ours."

*

My father had enjoyed the excitement and the danger. He had felt alive in this countryside with such close proximity to death. He had successfully navigated the battlefield and its horrors only to lose his way later in the mundane tasks of peace. I realised then why he had never boasted of what he had done, because he had not found it hard to do. It was ordinary life that he found difficult to understand.

But why did he never return to say thank you? He came back to Italy in 1950 on his honeymoon and again in 1972 with me and my sister. When I read my mother's account of that holiday I discovered with dismay that the two of them had come back here to look for the cave but had failed to stop to find the de Gregorios.

It was at the end of the holiday after my sister had gone on to Turkey and I had been deposited on a plane back to prep school in England. My parents drove back home on their own. They travelled up the Adriatic coast and my mother's diary describes how they drove to Roccascalegna to search for the cave on Tuesday 21st September 1972.

> *Early bathe and drove to Sangro and up into the hills to find cave. Had lunch by sea and sand dunes and then on to Rocascalanir [sic] and walked down overgrown paths to rocky stream where Dick searched and found his cave.*
>
> *Photos taken and walked back to find Donato's broken hut, drive in vain and getting dark, had desperate search for a camp site;*

at last found a level place high up above coast and fell into bed,
supperless.

No mention of wanting to find the de Gregorios. The most chari-
table explanation I can come up with is that my father believed
Donato to be dead and saw no purpose in contacting the rest of the
family. The photos have since been lost.

We returned to Alfonso's apartment and sat silently under
the fan with another round of limoncello; the failure of my father
to reach out weighed on me. I could see how much Alfonso had
longed for the chance to understand with his own eyes that my father had survived. To see him standing in front of him now would
be to know that the sacrifice they had made had not been in vain.

The family had waited 53 years – half a century – before making the video, hoping I suppose that he might turn up one day. I
could tell that my arrival had not fully closed the gap.

"I am heartbroken that my father never returned to Gessopalena to find you," I said rather lamely, "He was old and –"

"But he did," interrupted Alfonso.

I looked at him, not understanding.

"He did come back to try to find us. Maria and I were in the
village the summer that your parents came by in 1972."

I was stunned. I had no idea that Alfonso even knew we'd
come to Italy that year.

"After going to the cave, your parents went up to the farmhouse. When they found that it was in ruins, they drove up here to
Gessopalena to look for us."

"How do you know this, Alfonso?"

"Well, they asked the first person they saw in the street, 'Do
you know where Alfonso de Gregorio lives?' Unfortunately this
person happened to be my younger cousin. He was a taxi driver
at the time and he knew that we were in the village that day but he
lied, telling your parents that we were still living in Canada.

"You see, he didn't want them to go straight to me because

he was hoping to earn a bit of money driving your parents around in his taxi. Back then we used to get a number of British – and Germans – coming to look at the places where they had been in the war, and my cousin would offer to drive them around. But as soon as your parents heard that I was not here, they decided there was no point in staying and they drove away."

I gulped at my limoncello.

"When I heard what had happened," continued Alfonso, "I was so angry I never spoke to my cousin again. From that day to this I have not talked to him. In 30 years."

Later, I went back once more to my mother's red Woolworth's notebook and re-read the entry for that day. I realised that I had misread her faded pencil scrawl: "walked back to find Donato's broken hut" was actually, "walked back to find Donato's brother".

I felt some relief – and even greater disappointment for Alfonso. My father had made one attempt to connect. I imagined my parents standing in the main street of Gessopalena asking directions, my father in his old khaki shorts and my mother with her faded floppy hat, the kind that cricket umpires used to wear, both so transparently British. Gessopalena was not on any tourist map; the entire village must have recognised their purpose immediately. They had been within a few hundred yards of Alfonso's house.

*

Shortly after that summer, I had a dream about my father. In it, my brother, sister and I were on a bicycling holiday in Italy when we stopped to get a drink of water in a small mountain village. As we were standing admiring the view our tour guide said there was an English lecturer living nearby who had an interesting story to tell about the area. A local boy was sent to find him and when he appeared, we saw that the man was Dad. He was dressed immaculately in a pinstripe suit and looked fit and well.

"Where are you living?" we asked him. We assumed he was at home in England. He was younger than I could ever remember seeing him, even in my childhood. He seemed very content.

"I am back in the cave," he replied. I wondered how he could look so smart while he was living in a cave.

"Why?" I asked.

"I needed to pay off some debts," he replied and smiled.

ACKNOWLEDGEMENTS

My father is the central figure of this book, but it was my mother who played the leading role in my childhood. She endured the war and had to battle against a number of private losses and sorrows, yet the unconditional love and attention that she showed to her six children and step-children never wavered. Any talent I have as a parent with my children is due to the example that she set. She was a remarkable woman and I feel very privileged to have been her son.

I owe a debt of thanks to several people without whom this book would not have got off the ground: to Katty my wife who provided continuous encouragement and support; to Rebecca Nicolson my dear friend and publisher and to my two editors, Aurea Carpenter and Sarah Blake, a distinguished author in her own right. The persistent efforts that Antonio Lannutti made down the years to maintain the link between his family, the de Gregorios, and mine were remarkable. He is a source of fascinating stories and a delightful travelling companion.

My siblings, Rex, Chris, Kate, Alice and Liz, have all been supportive of this project, for which I'm very grateful.

This book is a personal history, the main sources for which were my father's own diaries and accounts, letters in the author's possession, my own notes and diaries and the memories of the de Gregorio family. I am deeply indebted to the unpublished first hand account that Lt. Colonel Tony MacDonnell, the 'Gloomy Dean', wrote of his escape in Italy and which he subsequently gave to my father. Tony MacDonnell appears not to have left any direct descendants; I have tried to locate his surviving relatives without success but perhaps this book will restore the connection.

David Montgomery, 2nd Viscount Montgomery of El Alamein, generously allowed letters written by his father to be quoted. Nigel Hamilton, the author of the three official biographies of Monty, pointed me in the direction of several key documents and provided some useful hints on writing about a subject on which he is a world authority. I am grateful to Roderick Suddaby, the Keeper of the Department of Documents at the Imperial War Museum, for sharing his time and his encyclopaedic knowledge about Monty and POW issues. The Museum contains a number of letters in the Montgomery collection that mention my father. The Army Personnel Centre in Glasgow was very efficient in providing copies of my father's service file.

The account of Jimmy Jones' crash in the desert comes from James Holland's 'Second World War Forum', which contains a first person description by Jimmy Jones. Details about MI9's activities came from the MI9 War Office Records in the National Archives and the semi-official history of MI9 entitled *MI9, Escape & Evasion 1939-1945* by MRD Foot and JM Langley, which also happens to be one of the few books written about that branch of Military Intelligence.

Camp PG49 at Fontanellato is mentioned in a number of accounts written by former POWs. The most comprehensive is *Home by Christmas* by Ian English and the thinly fictionalised *The Cage* by Dan Billany & David Dowie. I am also indebted to the classic *Love & War in the Apennines* by Eric Newby who was interned at Fontanellato at the same time as my father. The POW papers held by the Monte San Martino Trust was a useful source and two former PG 49 prisoners, Anthony Laing and Jack Clarke, provided a detailed description of their time in the camp and subsequent adventures to the *Birmingham Post*. The list of inmates at Fontanellato which appears at the back of the book comes from *Home By Christmas*.

Finally, I owe a debt of thanks to Clara Bingham, Alex Cadell, Jay Carney and Claire Shipman for reading early drafts, Martina Bagnoli and Giuseppe Zampaglione for their guidance, Nancy Delston, for showing me how to understand my father, Pietro Schechter for great friendship and the support of a fellow writer, Lucian Robinson my researcher, and Alex and David for providing a place to stay in Italy. Any errors are of course my own.

A NOTE ON THE MONTE SAN MARTINO TRUST

The Monte San Martino Trust was founded by former POWs to repay some of their debt to the Italian families who guided them to safety in the War and to honour their bravery and compassion. For twenty years the Trust has provided bursaries to young Italians to give them a chance to study in the UK. Many of the students are descendants of the contadini families who assisted the POWs. The Trust serves as a repository of manuscripts of former POWs and organises "freedom trails" for the children and grandchildren of the POWs to walk the routes that the POWs took while on the run through the stunning landscape of the Apennines. It can be contacted at www.msmtrust.org.uk

INDEX